MW00345869

Jacob Summerlin: King of the Crackers

Joe A. Akerman, Jr. and J. Mark Akerman

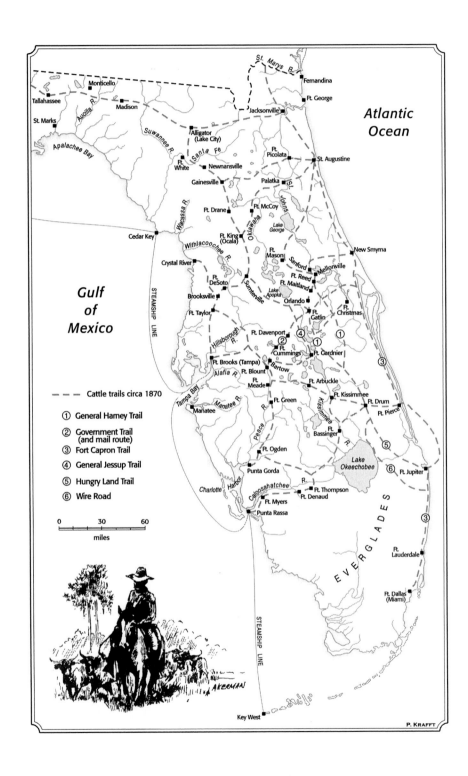

Atlantic
Ocean

Gulf
of
Mexico

- - - - Cattle trails circa 1870

① General Harney Trail
② Government Trail
(and mail route)
③ Fort Capron Trail
④ General Jessup Trail
⑤ Hungry Land Trail
⑥ Wire Road

0   30   60
miles

Monticello
Tallahassee
St. Marks
Madison
Aucilla R.
Apalachee Bay
Suwannee R.
Alligator
(Lake City)
Ft. White
Santa Fe
Newnansville
Gainesville
Wacassa R.
Ft. Drane
Cedar Key
Withlacoochee R.
Crystal River
Ft. King
(Ocala)
Ft. DeSoto
Brooksville
Ft. Taylor
Oklawaha
Sumterville
Hillsborough R.
Ft. Davenport
Ft. Cummings
Ft. Brooks (Tampa)
Ft. Blount
Alafia R.
Ft. Meade
Manatee R.
Manatee
Tampa Bay
Peace R.
Ft. Green
Ft. Ogden
Punta Gorda
Charlotte Harbor
Caloosahatchee R.
Ft. Myers
Punta Rassa
Ft. McCoy
St. Marys R.
Fernandina
Ft. George
Jacksonville
Ft. Picolata
St. Augustine
Palatka
St. Johns R.
Lake
George
Ft. Masoni
Sanford
Mellonville
New Smyrna
Ft. Reed
Ft. Maitland
Lake
Apopka
Orlando
Ft. Gatlin
Ft. Christmas
Ft. Gardnier
Bartow
Ft. Arbuckle
Ft. Kissimmee
Kissimmee R.
Ft. Drum
Ft. Pierce
Ft. Bassinger
Lake
Okeechobee
Ft. Jupiter
Ft. Thompson
Ft. Denaud
EVERGLADES
Ft. Lauderdale
Ft. Dallas
(Miami)
STEAMSHIP LINE
STEAMSHIP LINE
Key West
AKERMAN
P. KRAFFT

Jacob Summerlin: King of the Crackers

by

Joe A. Akerman, Jr. and J. Mark Akerman

Jacob Summerlin: King of the Crackers

Copyright 2004 by Joe A. Akerman, Jr. and J. Mark Akerman

Published by the Florida Historical Society Press (2004)

ISBN 10: 1-886104-16-6
ISBN 13: 978-1-886104-16-7

The Florida Historical Society Press
435 Brevard Avenue
Cocoa, FL 32922
http://myfloridahistory.org/fhspress

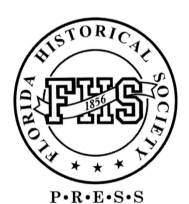

P•R•E•S•S

Table of Contents

Dedication

Angie

for her grace and goodness

Amy

for being a wonderful daughter and sister

and

Cole and Emma

our future generation

Preface

Although short, this biography was a long time in the writing. Its genesis came from a remarkable old photograph that used to hang in the old Orange County Court House in the 1940s. On my way home from Orlando High School, I often went out of my way to gaze at this fascinating picture of an old time Florida cowman, Jake Summerlin. Dressed in range clothes with a large bandana and a turned-back Stetson, he clutched a bullwhip in one hand and had a corncob pipe in his mouth—the epitome of a cracker cattleman. Some members of his family insisted that this was not a picture of Summerlin, presumably because of the pipe. He did not smoke. However, one need only compare this photograph with others made of him during his lifetime to see that this truly was Jake Summerlin. The pipe was probably only a prop.

The research and composition of this biography was a joint effort between my son, Joseph Mark Akerman, and myself. From the beginning of our inquiry into Summerlin's genealogy and life, we found significant discrepancies in the information published about this remarkable man. Descendants and historians tend to define this extraordinary man in different ways. In researching the story of Jake Summerlin's life, we spent a great deal of time dissecting these differences and seeking the "truth." We feel that our portrait of his life and character are accurate.

Some information that might have shed more light on Jacob Summerlin's life was not available to us. In particular, the biography probably would have been more complete if we had been able to locate the notes of the late historian and writer, Dena Snodgrass of Jacksonville. Snodgrass was a close friend of Jacob Summerlin's son, Samuel, who provided her with a lot of information about his father. It was our understanding that these papers were donated to the Smathers Library at the University of Florida; however, there was only limited material there on Summerlin. Hopefully these notes will surface at a later date. Certainly Jacob Summerlin deserves a more detailed and extensive portrait of his life than the one provided here. It is our wish that this book will inspire another expanded edition.

Joe A. Akerman, Jr.   J. Mark Akerman

i

Acknowledgements

Many kind people have encouraged and aided us in the course of researching and writing this biography of Jacob Summerlin, Jr. We are especially grateful for the assistance given to us by Kyle VanLandingham of Denver, Colorado, and by Canter Brown of Florida A&M University, probably the most prolific writer of Florida history today.

Special thanks should also go to Joe Knetsch of the Department of Environmental Protection, James M. Denham of Florida Southern College, Gary R. Mormino of the University of South Florida-St. Petersburg, Lewis N. Wynne, Executive Director of the Florida Historical Society, Robert Taylor, Florida Institute of Technology and president of Florida Historical Society, David Proctor of North Florida Community College and Cecil A. Tucker, II, Florida cattle rancher and writer.

If it had not been for the impatient spirit of John Maguire, former vice-president of North Florida Community College, this biography probably would not have been written. He constantly urged us, "to get on with it."

We would also like to thank Laura C. Brown of the Academic Affairs Library at the University of North Carolina who provided us with copies of personal letters from the Civil War and Angela Akerman who patiently typed the manuscript. Thanks to Brad Hutcheson for assistance with graphic work.

Thanks also to Sheila Hiss, Director of Library Services at North Florida Community College and to her staff: Kathy Sale, Kathy Smith, Kay Boatright, Marie Waldrop and Linda Brown. We especially appreciate their patience and research skills. There is not a more professional staff in the state.

The archivists at the Florida State Archives in Tallahassee, Joan Morris, David Coles, Adam Watson and Boyd Murphree were also extremely helpful during our research. A special thanks also to Anna Fertic Bronson who gave us access to the Bronson Family papers.

Summerlin family members, such as Jan Miller of Fort Pierce and Tommie S. Ferrell of Perry also provided us with information and family papers, which proved very useful. Other generous people such as Zack Waters of Rome, Georgia, and Sara Nell Gran of Fort Myers supplied us with pictures and newspaper articles about Jacob Summerlin. The late Louise Frisbee of Bartow was also gracious enough to furnish us with copies of a long series of articles she wrote about the Summerlins.

Tim Sanders, County Clerk of Madison County was kind enough to track down data from Orange, Polk and Hillsborough counties concerning Jacob Summerlin's estate which also was very useful.

Lastly thanks must be given to Edward F. Keuchel of Florida State University. His book, *A History of Columbia County*, was extremely useful because the county records that covered the early years of Summerlin's life in Columbia County were destroyed when the courthouse burned.

Summerlin Family

1) Joseph Summerlin married Sarh Mccarty

2) Jacob Summerlin
Married 1st Lydia Lang
Married 2nd mary ann Hagen, 2-8-1821

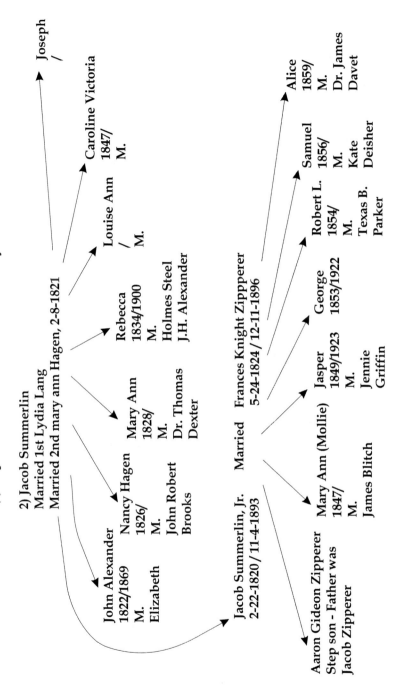

Joseph /

Caroline Victoria
1847/
M.

Louise Ann
/
M.

Rebecca
1834/1900
M.
Holmes Steel
J.H. Alexander

Mary Ann
1828/
M.
Dr. Thomas
Dexter

Nancy Hagen
1826/
M.
John Robert
Brooks

John Alexander
1822/1869
M.
Elizabeth

Jacob Summerlin, Jr.   Married   Frances Knight Zippperer
2-22-1820 / 11-4-1893   5-24-1824 / 12-11-1896

Alice
1859/
M.
Dr. James
Davet

Samuel
1856/
M.
Kate
Deisher

Robert L.
1854/
M.
Texas B.
Parker

George
1853/1922

Jasper
1849/1923
M.
Jennie
Griffin

Mary Ann (Mollie)
1847/
M.
James Blitch

Aaron Gideon Zipperer
Step son - Father was
Jacob Zipperer

iii

Chapter 1

Roots and Early Childhood

Jacob Summerlin, Junior (1820 - 1893) was in many ways the essence of what Frederick Jackson Turner defined as the "true American," one whose character was largely shaped by the challenge and struggle for survival on the American frontier. But Summerlin's true *persona* is not so simply characterized. He was more complex than Turner's frontiersman. While his individualism, his courage, his resourcefulness and his emotional and physical strengths were representative of Turner's successful frontier original, he was endowed with a strong philanthropic spirit, a sturdy moral tenacity and an incredible modesty. Along with a keen wit, he seemed to have a true sense of reality — never taking himself too seriously and never, as he said, "putting on airs."[1] As a businessman, he was shrewd, but he was always fair and appreciated the needs of the poor and the powerless. An agrarian Andrew Carnegie in some ways — but as much in touch with the simple things in life as Henry David Thoreau.

Called "King of the Crackers" by some, he dearly loved what it implied, in his case, one careless of comfort and close to the earth. He is primarily remembered as a cattle baron who owned thousands of beeves that ranged over an area as large as the modern state of Israel, and as a philanthropist who donated money, land and cattle to support churches, schools, local governments and widows. But he was also a highly successful merchant and hosteler, an exporter, a veteran of three wars and an effective peacemaker.

One of Jacob Summerlin, Junior's earliest ancestors was a Scotch merchant from Edinburgh or Gladstaine, Scotland, named John Somervaille. *Summerlin* has had a number of spellings down through the years — all of which have produced a nightmare for family genealogists. One of the first spellings in America was Summerell, but the name has also appeared as Somerell, Somerwell, Sum-

---

[1] Frederick Jackson Turner, "The Significance of the American Frontier in American History," a speech given at the World's Columbian Exposition in 1893.

merland, Summerall, and Sumerlan. In 1845, Jacob Summerlin, Jake Summerlin's father, had the name legally changed to Summerlin and in this biography the legal spelling will be used.[2]

John Summerlin moved to America in the 1680s and in 1687 he patented 420 acres in Isle of Wight County, Virginia. He transported his family and nine other people to what was then tobacco tideland. John was married to Frances (last name uncertain) or to Margaret Winram, also a Scot. They had three sons, one of whom was Henry, who may have moved to Florida in his early years.

An interesting request made by John Summerlin appeared in the Wight County Court Records dated July 9, 1690. He asked John McLeland "to forgive him for having charged him for bewitching two of his children to death." Salem, Massachusetts, evidently was not the only place where beliefs in witchcraft existed in the seventeenth century.[3]

The Summerlin family was prolific, and by the last part of the eighteenth century, like many other Scots and Ulster Scots, the family was pretty well scattered over Virginia, the Carolinas, Georgia and eventually into Florida. Joseph Summerlin, son of John Summerlin and grandfather of Jacob Summerlin, Junior, moved to Florida in the 1780s with his wife, Sarah McCarty, to escape the wrath of the Regulators since Joseph was a Loyalist. After the American Revolutionary War formally ended in 1783, he served in one of Governor Tonyn's ranger companies. Their duty was to maintain order during the transitional period when Florida was being reoccupied by Spain. It was a time when Florida was rapidly becoming one of America's most turbulent frontiers, and Tonyn's Rangers were generally unsuccessful.

In 1792, Joseph Summerlin acquired two tracts of land of 200 and 150 acres as head rights — one tract was at Long Bluff on the St. Mary's River while the other was located at Wills Swamp (also known as Williams Creek), five miles from the mouth of the Nassau River. Starting a Summerlin tradition, he invested in livestock and undoubtedly branded wild scrub cattle that still roamed the woods. However, the family was forced to move in 1793 when the Spanish governor issued a proclamation directing all settlers on the west side of the St. Johns River to transfer to the east side, presumably because of the "French threat." Summerlin established a successful 300-acre plantation. But in 1812 Indians and the so-called Patriots of the Patriot War destroyed Summerlin's enterprise.[4] By 1816, Summerlin had settled on a vacant tract of land situated on a fork of Cormorant Branch and Julington Creek. Despite continued conflict with the Indians, Summerlin became fairly prosperous by developing an orange

---

[2]Papers of Jan Miller, "Descendants of James Somervaille," Fort Pierce, 2003-2004.

[3]*Ibid.*

[4]*Ibid.* Susan Parker Correspondence (Citation from *Spanish Land Grants* and *Loyalty Oaths from East Florida Papers*) St. Augustine: 20 Sept. 87.

grove and a small peach orchard—along with other fruit orchards. However, he "principally turned his attention to raising stocks of cattle and hogs of which he had usually a large number."[5]

In 1792, his wife Sarah gave birth to a son whom they named Jacob. He would become the father of Jacob or "Jake" Summerlin, Junior. Jacob was baptized on May 13, 1793, at St. Augustine by Father Thomas Hassett, a Catholic priest.[6]

There is little information about the older Jacob Summerlin's early years, but while he was still young, he served in a Spanish militia company along with his father, Joseph. Eventually he was classified as a "rebel" by the Spanish authorities. North Florida was then a hotbed of intrigue, brigandage, depredations, changing loyalties and Indian raids. There was nothing else like it in American history, not even on the Western frontier. The inability of Spain to protect this isolated outpost of their empire was the major cause of chaos.

Florida provided a refuge for runaway slaves from Georgia plantations, and Spain encouraged their immigration to Florida. But to white settlers, runaway slaves and even free African-Americans were considered fair game for capture and relocation in southern states. Robber bands operated freely from camps below the St. Mary's River, plundering plantations and stealing slaves who were "salable in Georgia." Jacob Summerlin and a close friend, Isaiah Hart, once seized a free black Florida family in 1811 and took them to Georgia where they were then sold as slaves.[7]

In 1812, Jacob was a guide for Lieutenant Colonel Thomas Smith, who led an invading force of Georgians into Florida, allegedly to punish Indians who were raiding farms and settlements north of the St. Mary's River. Later Jacob would declare, "[I] was hope full [sic] that [I] would be allowed to remain in peace, but the Spanish officer at the Cow Ford (later Jacksonville)...who commands Black troops ordered the negroes to Lay Hold of [me] for having been a Pilott [sic] in [the] expedition against the Indians." Summerlin was seized by a Don Justo Lopas and charged with treason, but he managed to escape across the St. Mary's River into Camden County, Georgia.[8]

Despite the fact that Jacob's father, Joseph, had apparently suffered at the

---

[5]Buchner Harris Papers, Georgia Department of Archives and History, Atlanta: Also cited in Canter Brown, *Ossian Bingley Hart*, (Baton Rouge: Louisiana State University Press, 1997), pp. 12, 13, 14; Richard K. Murdock, *The Georgia Florida Frontier, 1793-1796*, (Berkeley: University of California Press, 1951) p. 6.

[6]Brown, *Hart*, pp. 10-11; Jan Miller, Papers regarding Jacob Summerlin, Senior's baptism in St. Augustine, May 13, 1793.

[7]Harris Papers, *Ibid.*

[8]Canter Brown, Hart, p. 13; Rembert Patrick, *Florida Fiasco: Rampant Rebels on the Georgia-Florida Border, 1810-1815* (Athens, GA: University of Georgia Press, 1954), p. 283, p. 302; Harris Papers, *Ibid.*

hands of the Patriots, Jacob later joined the invaders in their attempt to form an East Florida Republic and sue to become a territory of the United States. A petition requesting admission into the Union for the self-proclaimed Republic of East Florida was sent from Fort Mitchell on January 25, 1814, to the U.S. Congress. Jacob Summerlin Senior's name, along with that of one hundred and four "Citizens of the District of Elotchaway [sic]," appeared in the document. Apparently, the petition did not reach Washington, and there were no further attempts to establish an East Florida Republic.[9] In time, avenging Indians and fugitive slaves drove many of the Patriots back to the St. Mary's River. In his biography of Ossian Bingley Hart, Canter Brown points out that the Patriot War devastated East Florida causing many Patriots to become "wanderers."[10] However, a number of the individuals who signed the petition recovered their losses and became influential leaders in northeast Florida and southeast Georgia. One of these was Jacob Summerlin, Senior. After the collapse of the East Florida Republic scheme, Summerlin accepted a pardon offered by the Spanish governor because as he stated, "I was in an 'imbarrassed [sic] circumstances.'"

In the summer of 1816, Zephaniah Kingsley, along with Henry Young and George Clarke, worked out a plan to establish order in northeast Florida by dividing the area between the St. Johns and St. Mary's Rivers into three districts. Desperate to bring stability to the area, the Spanish authorities agreed to the plan. In essence, this created an unofficial East Florida Republic, in fact if not in name, with the consent of Spain.

While in Camden County, Jacob Summerlin courted and married Lydia Lang, a relative of his friend, David Lang, who had also been a part of the East Florida filibustering effort.[11] Lydia and Jacob had two boys—the first was Joseph and the second was probably Jacob, Junior, the subject of this biography and referred to hereafter as "Jake." There are questions about whom young Jacob's biological mother was, but if the birth dates in the Summerlin Family Bible and on his tombstone are correct, he was born in 1820. At that time Lydia and Jacob were married. Lydia Lang died in 1820(?) and on February 8, 1821, Jacob Senior remarried—this time to Mary Ann Hagen also of Camden County, Georgia. Hagen was a direct descendant of William Cone, known as the "Fighting Parson," who rode with and preached to General Francis Marion's volunteers dur-

[9]Jean H. Mizell, *Founding Pioneers and Their Descendants*. RootsWeb.com or Ancestry.com quick search. Updated Nov. 24, 2003. Charlton W. Tebeau, *A History of Florida*, (Miami: University of Miami Press, 1971) pp. 107, 108; James W. Covington, *The Seminoles of Florida*, University Press of Florida (Gainesville: University Presses of Florida, 1993), pp. 28, 29; Canter Brown, *Florida's Peace River Frontier*. (Orlando: University of Central Florida Press, 1991) pp. 6-7, pp. 349-350; *Papers of Revolution of East Florida*, Bundle 112H9, Microcopy, Roll #42, Florida State Archives, Tallahassee, FL.

[10]Jan Miller Papers.

[11]Mizell, *Ibid*.

ing the last years of the Revolutionary War.[12]

Sometime between 1821 and 1825, Jacob and Mary left Camden County, Georgia, for Mandarin, Florida. They eventually moved to Alachua County and settled near the old Indian settlement of Alligator. The couple appeared on the 1830 census for Alachua County, an area that would become a part of Columbia County in 1832.[13] This is where Jake spent most of his early life. Alligator Town, originally an Indian village, was deserted when the Summerlins moved there, but as late as 1813, there had been sixty or seventy Indian families living in this immediate area. When an early settler, Enoch Daniels, visited the area in 1818, he said the village was deserted. Chief Alligator (Halpatter Tustenaggee) abandoned the site and led his tribe south when Colonel John Williams invaded North Florida in late 1813 with a group of Tennessee volunteers.

A traveler to Lake Alligator in 1824 noted that the only persons living nearby were "old man Edwards and two men named Austeen [Osteen]." But after Florida became a U.S. Territory in 1821, a steady influx of settlers from Georgia and the Carolinas moved into the area. The 1830 United States Census listed twenty-seven households in the Alligator community.[14] Most of those who came brought little with them except, perhaps, a wagon, a musket, a meager supply of tools, and clothes.

Like many Florida frontier communities, Alligator Town would have its name changed several times. According to George G. Keen in *Cracker Times and Pioneer Lives*, the tiny community was actually named Alligator by a Methodist circuit rider, James Pearce, in honor of an earlier chief commander of the Seminole Indians in the area. Captain Jacob Summerlin, who eventually owned all the property known as Alligator, wanted a more dignified name and renamed the town Lancaster, in honor of a fellow Whig and circuit judge of the Florida Eastern Circuit, Joseph B. Lancaster. Since Summerlin owned the land, the name change became a *fait accompli*. In 1858, ten years after Summerlin's death, former U.S. Congressman James M. Baker moved to Lancaster:

> When James M. Baker came back to frontier life, full of refined memories, he cast about him for a new name for his adopted hometown, and then it took very naturally to the name of Lake City on account of the lakes in Captain Summerlin's fields.

---

[12]*Ibid.*

[13]Unpublished Census Schedules, Fifth Census, 1830, National Archives Microfil M19, Reel 15, Alachua County; Edward F. Keuchel, *A History of Columbia County Florida* (Lake City: Hunter Printing, 1996), p. 24.

[14]Keuchel, *Ibid.*

Other men of influence sanctioned the new name, and so it was changed to Lake City, which it has remained since.[15]

The area where the Summerlins settled was not part of Florida's plantation belt nor identified with what has become known as the Red Hills of Middle Florida, which included Madison, Jefferson, Gadsden, Leon and Jackson counties. For one thing, the terrain and soil did not lend itself well to plantation cash crop operations. Cotton became an important money crop, but the land was simply not as productive as that west of the Suwannee River. The area around Alligator and in much of Columbia County was "poor pine and palmetto." "The soil has been described as *spodosois*, poorly drained sandy soils with dark sandy subsoil layers. Much of it was underlain by phosphate limestone." Still, there were seemingly unending stands of virgin yellow pines, some over one hundred and twenty feet high and over forty inches in diameter at waist level. Dry hardwood hammocks filled with persimmon, oaks, gum, maple and cherry, and cypress bay heads that punctuated the pinelands provided some forage, firewood, construction materials and salable lumber. Seminole Indians often inhabited the larger hammocks. Crystal clear lakes, full of fish and bordered by cypress and bay trees, were clustered near the tiny community of Alligator. A farmer needed to dig only a few feet to hit the water table for drinking and cooking water. The woods were full of wild game and herds of wild, unbranded scrub cattle descended from the *criolla* or Spanish breeds.[16]

The land was not without its beauty. Although generally flat, there were some gently rolling hills and the lack of variation in topography was made up by the wide diversity of flora of every imaginable color, size and shape. During the fall, maple and gum trees presented beautiful shades of red, yellow and orange, which were especially vivid and intense against the expanses of green pine, live oak and grey cypress. "In those days of virgin timber, everything was pretty much as God made it."

Occasional homesteads were scattered miles apart. The texture of the dwellings and barns hardly seemed to break the landscape. Durable and unpretentious, they reflected the nature of their inhabitants. Forrest McDonald and Grady McWhiney described them as "nothing more than transplanted Highlanders," who had traded their bagpipes for country fiddles, "while keeping alive the contradictory mix of qualities—easygoing yet proud, clannish but elaborately polite and hospitable—that have made them so creative and intrat-

---

[15]James M. Denham and Canter Brown, Junior, *Cracker Times and Pioneer Lives,* (Columbia: University of South Carolina Press, 2000), pp. 57-58.

[16]Keuchel, *Ibid., p. 60.*Joe A. Akerman, *Florida Cowman, A History of the Florida Cattle Industry,* (Kissimmee: Florida Cattleman's Association, 1999), p. 37; Frederick Davis, "A View of East Florida in 1817," *The Florida Historical* Quarterly, XIX, October 1940, pp. 155-162.

able."[17] Many of the ancestors of these Celtic settlers left Britain for Philadelphia, then spread south and west along the Appalachians, sometimes spilling over into the Piedmont and even into the flatlands of the Carolinas, Georgia and Florida. Some of the earliest pioneers of Columbia County were the Browns, Burnetts, Clarks, Collins, Douglasses, Hamiltons, Hunters, McClellans, Mahons, Montgomerys, Moores, the Osteens, Rosses, Williamsons and the Woods — all descended from earlier Scots and Ulster-Scots.[18]

Except for Indian and wagon trails, there were no real roads running north and south near the Summerlin homestead. However, there was a north-south trail marked by ax cuts that ran from Newnansville through Alligator into Georgia. About thirty miles directly south from Alligator was the Bellamy road, which ran from St. Augustine to Tallahassee. It opened in 1826, but it was a poor excuse for a road, even by territorial standards. Built by John Bellamy of Jefferson County, it averaged about twelve feet in width and generally followed the old Spanish Road that connected the early Franciscan missions or *doctrinas*. Throughout Florida, including Columbia County, water was the preferred mode of transportation. But the Summerlins used parts of the Bellamy Road to travel to Jacksonville, and when Jacob Summerlin served in the Territorial Legislature or had business in Tallahassee, he traveled over parts of this road. During the territorial days, 1821-1845, there was a route from Jacksonville to Alligator by which a mail coach traveled once a week. Part of this mail route was probably the Bellamy Road. One stop on this line was the Moses Barber plantation.[19]

When the Summerlins established roots at Alligator, there were four children, Jake's younger brother, John, his older brother, Joseph, and an older sister, Nancy. Although there is little information about the family during their early years in what was then Alachua County, they were a close-knit family. The brothers, almost the same age, were tied together by a close work ethic. Although Jacob Summerlin was relatively well off and owned approximately 300 acres, all of the family members were constantly driven to improve their economic circumstances. Besides the land the Summerlins and other settlers could put into crop production, of course, there was almost limitless land for pasturing cattle and other livestock. Some writers portrayed the so-called Florida crackers as indolent and slothful, but most were not and spent the greater part of their waking hours working, for subsistence or for self- improvement.

By the 1830s, Columbia County was a hotbed of violence as conflicts between

[17]Jerry Adler and Holly Morris, "Celts vs. Anglo-Saxons," *Newsweek*, August 10, 1981, p.70.

[18]Keuchel, *Ibid.*

[19]Denham and Brown, *CrackerTimes*, p. 114; Joe Akerman, "The Old Spanish Trail," Tallahassee *Democrat*, June 18, 1976.

Indians and settlers worsened. "Around the Sandlin estate 20 Indians were killed trying to steal corn. Twenty more were killed on an island in a swamp near Ocean Pond." It was estimated that a force of 400 Indians was encamped between Ocean Pond (near Alligator) and the Okefenokee Swamp. In the summer of 1835, George G. Keen, a journalist and early resident of Columbia County, reported that there was a "great commotion in the neighborhood of Alligator which cannot be described. The Indians was [sic] all over this country and there was no place of refuge for the whites...The people were going in every direction and not one of them knowing the way where they wanted to go to...the people were running from the Indians that was [sic] in one direction, often times would run into a bunch of Indians that was [sic] in another direction."[20]

Jacob Summerlin took a part of his family to nearby Newnansville, which was overflowing with refugees but was fairly well protected. He sent or took his wife, Mary Ann, to Jefferson County where she resided with her mother and several other relatives. Sadly, Mary Ann died shortly after in February 1836. Her obituary noted that "the community in which she resided sustained an almost irreparable loss. In the bosom of a fond husband and obedient children there is an aching void which can never be filled. As a child, a mother, and a wife, she was devoted — as a Christian her light shown as a brilliant star in the midst of a dark and benighted land — her candle was not hid, but shown in the splendor of a glorious religion. Mrs. Summerlin bore her affliction with patience and resignation."[21]

Mary Ann Summerlin was thirty-one years old at the time of her death. While still young, she had a powerful influence on the lives of her children. Writer and journalist D.B. McKay would later say that Jake "had the iron of Calvinism in his soul."[22] His life demonstrated many of the values and virtues he acquired from his mother.

It is difficult to say how much of Jake's character was shaped by his father. They both had a mutual interest in public service. The older Summerlin was very much involved in state politics and served east Florida in both the Senate and the House of Legislative Council. He was a dedicated Whig and was very much opposed to the territory becoming a state in the 1830s. In 1842, he also supported a plan for establishing a separate territory of East Florida — an anathema to the Democrats of Middle Florida who feared that East Florida would become an abolitionist territory. Interestingly, the question of moving the capital of Florida from Tallahassee to a location farther south had already surfaced,

---

[20]Denham and Brown, *Ibid.*, pp. 28-29; *The Florida Index*, 1899, pp. 70-71, 81.

[21]Mary Hagen Summerlin, Obituary, *Tallahassee Floridian*, 20 Feb. 1836.

[22]D.B. McKay, *Pioneer Florida*, p. 327; Joe Akerman, "Jacob Summerlin: King of the Crackers," in *Florida Pathfinders*. (Saint Leo, FL: Saint Leo College Press, 1994), p. 105.

but Summerlin helped defeat a resolution that would have made this possible. Jacob Summerlin also served as a justice of the peace in Alachua County and was appointed to the important post of appraiser for the First Union Bank of Florida by Governor Duval. Since this was Florida's most important bank at the time, Summerlin was in a powerful position to influence the development and growth of Columbia County and east Florida.[23]

Years later, Jake also would serve in a number of political and public ways— usually on the local level. In Hillsborough County, he served as a justice of the peace, deputy sheriff, road commissioner and postmaster. While living in Orlando, he was elected president of the town council and facilitated a proposal for making Orlando the county seat of Orange County by using his own cash![24]

Both men were excellent businessmen and welcomed commercial challenges. Jake, though not as literate as his father, seemed to be more compassionate, generous and public spirited. "He was an internal man in many ways to whom ideas were more interesting than things."[25] In time he would become rich, respected, even revered, but he always preferred to dress and live simply. He derived great joy from his sizeable family, his many friends, his success in solving problems and, especially, from his acts of benevolence. Regardless of what activity or business venture he was involved in, whether it involved mercantilism, hostelry or milling, he could always find solace in the saddle while cow hunting, soldiering or simply traveling.

Jake had no formal education, but he could read and write legibly. His favorite book, which he read many times, was *Livingston in Africa*, an adventurous account of the famous Dr. Livingston who ministered to people in Africa and sought to find the headwaters of the great Nile River. No doubt Jake identified with Livingston's boldness, intrepidity and his great humility. How important are the books that young people read! A reporter once described Jake as having "a PhD in every kind of survival and his lack of education was perfectly balanced by his common sense and intuition."[26]

There are a number of anecdotes about Jake's early years. D.B. McKay wrote

---

[23]Clarence Carter, *Territorial Papers of the United States*, Vol. XXIV, 13 Feb. 1834, pp. 966-968.

[24]Hillsborough County Court House, Clerk of Circuit Court, Deed Book A., pp. 125, 155; Minutes Book A [1846-1863]; Florida Historical Records Survey, WPA, Roster of State and County Offices and Commissioners by the Governor's of Florida, 1845-1885, (Jacksonville: Feb. 1941), p. 145; Quintilla Geer Bruton and David E. Baily, (Winston-Salem, NC: Hunter Publishing Co. 1984); *U.S. Post Office Dept. Records of Appointment, 1831-1971, Florida*, M841, Roll #20 [Hernando-Okeechobee Counties] N.A. Florida State Archives, Tallahassee, FL; Louise Frisbie "Jacob Summerlin, Part II," *The Democrat and Leader*, Nov. 11, 1973.

[25]Joe Akerman, "Jacob Summerlin, Cattle King and Philanthropist," Paper given at Florida Historical Society Annual Meeting, Daytona, May 1999.

[26]McKay; Devane, "Biographical Sketch of Jacob Summerlin," *Bartow Advance Courier*, May 25, 1887.

that by the time he was seven years old; he could ride a horse and crack a whip as well as any cow hunter. Another biographer claimed that by his early teens, Jake could read a trail like an Indian and that he had no peers when it came to breaking a horse. Later events in his life gave credence to some of these claims, but one bit of lore about him that overmatched any feat claimed by Davy Crockett or even Paul Bunyan, was that he could "de-wing" a fly with a cow whip at a distance of eighteen feet. His exceptional skills at tracking and trailing were acquired from the Seminoles with whom he hunted and played during his childhood.[27]

During his teenage years, north Florida became a very dangerous place in which to live because of conflicts between Seminole Indians and settlers over land and grazing rights. After the Moultrie Creek Treaty of 1823, Florida Indians were restricted to a four million acre reservation in the middle of the state. Forced to give up their cattle, cut off from the sea and expected to feed themselves through subsistence farming, many Seminoles left the reservation and drifted back to their old hunting grounds. Numerous bands roamed the woods near the Summerlin homestead. In the early territorial days there were only a handful of white settlers in this area, and there was little competition for the use of rangeland and the access to hunting habitats. But occasionally a small band of Creeks or Seminoles would steal some cattle or slaves or even kill a settler. Most settlers had already experienced some conflict with Native Americans before coming to Florida, and they were frightened of further Indian hostilities. As early as 1825, Jacob Summerlin was a co-signer of a written complaint sent to the U.S. Secretary of War directed toward "Semenole [sic] Indians stealing and hunting through the County (then Alachua County) in large parties contrary to the treaty made and entered into between the United States Commission and the Seminole Indians in September, 1823...[c]ommitting depredations on the stock of cattle and hogs and robbing the plantations, and enticing away their slaves." A similar petition, also co-signed by Summerlin, Senior, was addressed to President John Quincy Adams two years later.[28] Attacks on and atrocities committed against settlers increased all over east and middle Florida in late 1826. The Seminoles also suffered from violence by settlers and the brother of the Mikasuki Chief, Tiger Tail, died from a lashing ordered by a local justice of the peace.[29]

Like most yeoman farmers in the area, the Summerlin family also owned a

---

[27]W.D. Shilling, *Polk Lore*, 3 March 68; D.B. McKay, *Pioneer Florida*, Southern Publishing Co., p. 327. *Florida Times Union*, September 25, 1883, p. 3.

[28]Memorial to U.S. President, Clarence Carter, *Territorial Papers*, Vol. XXIII, (March 6, 1826), pp. 462-463.

[29]Keuchel, 34, cited from Jerrell H. Shofner, *History of Jefferson County* (Tallahassee: 1976), pp. 34-35.

number of cattle and hogs that ranged unfettered, sometimes identified by brands and even ear crops. The Indians living in the area viewed the wild woods cattle in the same way that the tribes of the Great Plains looked upon the buffalo. But when an Indian slaughtered a cow claimed by a settler, there was invariably a dispute that often resulted in violence.

George G. Keen, in the *Florida Index*, related a rumor about Summerlin and the conflict he had with the Indians over cattle in early 1835:

> I heard the men say the Indians was stealing cattle south of Alligator and the cattle they were stealing belonged to Jacob Summerlin [Senior] and Jack Hope. This report was current in the northern part of Columbia County. Understand and mistake me not; I don't [vouch] for the validity of this report.
>
> The next report that reached us was that Summerlin and Hope killed every Indian that they caught alone in the woods. Pretty soon another report reache[d] us that Summerlin and Hope caught two Indians butchering a cow of Summerlins' and they..., on June 18, 1835, tied them up and gave them a dose of hickory oil. The men in our neighborhood said that would bring war.[30]

While little was done to enforce the 1823 treaty, there was a growing movement already underway to move all the Florida Indians from the Florida territory to the West. When Andrew Jackson was elected president in 1828, the removal of the Seminole Indians and the other "civilized nations" was one of his chief priorities. In 1834, the Senate ratified the Payne's Landing and the Fort Gibson treaties which gave Jackson, at least on paper, the go ahead to transfer the Florida Indians. A futile attempt by the Army to make the reluctant Seminoles leave led to the Second Seminole War, the longest continuous Indian war in American history.

Jake later recalled that on the eve of the Second Seminole War, he saw the great Seminole war leader Osceola and was very impressed with him. He said of him, "He was a noble man...manly looking and tall and straight, and you felt a sort of awe in his presence you couldn't shake off."[31]

A neighbor of the Summerlins, Mary Burnett, who lived at Newnansville during the Second Seminole War, described the relationship between the first white settlers in Northern Alachua County and the great Osceola and other Seminoles:

> For a time the Indians were friendly and good neighbors to the white people. Osceola, best known of the Indian leaders, often passed the Burnett family leaving presents of game and fruit, as he was on his way to Newnansville.

[30]Denham and Brown, *Cracker Times*, p. 27.

[31]Joe Akerman, *Florida Cowman*, p. 4.

11

Another Indian who was the express carrier from Palatka to Tallahassee slept in the Burnett kitchen one night each week. Realizing that the white people were encroaching on their lands, the Indians began to plot mischief by stealing cattle....[32]

Jake often felt ambivalent about the Indians. He seemed incapable of an enduring hatred against anyone and yet he volunteered and served in militia units throughout the Second Seminole War. Such was often the dilemma of the American frontiersman who had befriended Native Americans, but was forced to protect his home and family. Still later in his life, he demonstrated, on occasion, his compassion for Native Americans, and for a period after the Indian wars, he was only one of a few white Floridians that the Seminoles seemed to trust.

When Jacob and Frances Summerlin moved to the Ichepucksassa area in 1845 their living conditions were just as primitive as these; however, their early home site had not been clear-cut by loggers. (Florida State Photographic Archives)

---

[32]Mary Burnett, "Correspondence of Mrs. Mary Burnett, 1830-1840," Alachua County, Florida. (Copies held by Joe A. Akerman; Madison, FL).

Chapter 2

The Summerlins and the Second Seminole War

Conflicts between the settlers and the Indians increased in the mid-1830s in Columbia County and other parts of the territory. In June 1835, the year the Second Seminole War "officially" started, Jacob Summerlin and six other settlers encountered and overpowered an Indian hunting party near Hog Town (Gainesville). The braves were beaten with rawhide whips for hunting outside their reservation. "During the beating two other braves appeared and fired on the whites wounding three of them...One Indian was eventually killed and another was wounded before the fracas ended."[1]

Farther south on the military road from Fort Brooke to Fort King, Private Kinsley H. Dalton, a courier for the Army, was killed while carrying mail to Fort King. Some Seminoles had agreed to move to the Oklahoma Territory. One of these, Chief Charley Emathla, who sold his cattle in November 1835 in preparation for departure, was killed near Wetumpka. Osceola and his followers allegedly committed the act. Cash from the cattle sale was scattered near his body to show that he was not killed for money.[2]

"Other incidents began to take place all over the Alachua area and beyond." Indian trails running from north Central Florida and Middle Florida to the Okefenokee Swamp ran through Alachua and Columbia counties, making homesteads near Alligator and much of the county particularly susceptible to Indian attacks. On December 17, 1835, the Summerlin homestead at Alligator was attacked, as were the plantations of Captain Simmons of Micanopy and of Captain Priest of Wacahouta. When news of the attack on the Simmons' home reached Fort Crum, then headquarters of the local militia, it brought a quick response. Captain Jacob Summerlin and a Captain Gibbons were dispatched with only a twenty-minute notice with orders to pursue and kill the Indians.

---

[1]Keuchel, *History of Columbia County*, p. 37; Cited from *Niles Register*, XLIX, 19 Dec. 1835, p. 235; John Mahon, *History of the Second Seminole War*. (Gainesville: University of Florida Press, 1967), pp. 98-101.

[2]Tebeau, *A History of Florida*, pp. 158-160.

Accompanied by J. Carr, one of the victims of the Indian attack, they trailed the warriors, but as so often happened, the Indians eluded them. Later Captain Priest's plantation at Wacahouta was attacked again and destroyed. The Indians seized all of Priest's horses and drove off twenty-one fine fat hogs. "Inhabitants every where [sic] in the neighborhood deserted their houses and fled, congregating together in temporary stockades. The situation in East Florida was extremely precarious during the early stages of the war." Except for a few months from 1835 to 1842, no white settlers were safe from Picolata on the St. Johns to Alligator and westward to the Suwannee River. "Joseph M. White reported in the U.S. Congress that he did not think that enough white men lived along the Alachua frontier to defend it adequately, even with the support of the regular army."

"In early December a baggage train traveling from Jacksonville to Micanopy was ambushed by some eighty warriors led by the remarkable Seminole war leader, Osceola. Six soldiers were killed and eight wounded. Attacks continued and by early June, 1836 the country between Newnansville (about twenty miles southeast of Alligator) and Black Creek to the east was reported to be devastated." Many settlers left their farms untended and crowded into Newnansville where the residents and refugees became so alarmed that women and children threw up defensive entrenchments, which were guarded mostly by boys and old men.[3] Most of the able bodied men along the Alachua frontier formed scouting companies to search for Seminole and Mikasuki encampments. "In September 1836, *Niles Register* reported that Fort Gilleland (Newnansville) was the last remaining post occupied by American troops between Black Creek and the Suwannee River and it was under attack."[4]

By 1837, seven forts had been constructed in the Columbia County area. One was at Alligator and named Fort Lancaster by Jacob Summerlin. Located at what is now the corner of Madison and Marion Streets, it was one of the first forts to be abandoned. There was also Fort White on the Santa Fe River, Fort Cass on the Suwannee River at White Springs, Fort Number 15 near High Springs, Fort 16 between Alligator and Columbia City, Fort 19 near present day Lulu and Fort Eagle, southwest of present day Live Oak.[5]

U.S. Army surgeon Jacob Rhett Motte, who served with the U.S. Army in Alachua County, noted the devastation caused by Indian raids, "As we approached Newnansville, the County Town of Alachua [County]...we here found fields of

---

[3]Keuchel, *History of Columbia County*, pp. 38-40; Cited from *Niles Register*, 2 May 1836, pp. 206-207; 28 May 1836, p. 217; 11 June 1836, p. 200; 2 July 1836; pp. 309-310; *The Tallahassee Floridian*, 17 Sept. 1836; *Niles Register*, 17 Sept. 1836, pp. 35-36.

[4]Mahon, *History of the Second Seminole War*, p. 175; John L. Williams, *The Territory of Florida*. Floridiana Facsimile. (Gainesville: University of Florida Press, 1962), p. 247.

[5]Keuchel, *History of Columbia County*, pp. 54-55.

tassell'd corn growing as it were 'upon their own hook;' for the houses of which the fields pertained were all abandoned by the owners through fear of savages."[6]

Before 1835, Newnansville was hardly more than a frontier way station. According to a resident, Mary Burnett, "The settlement consisted of a few crude dwellings, a court house and a bar room. There was little money and little use for it, for the people raised their own provisions and enough cotton, which was spun and woven at home for their clothing. Transportation was foot, horse and horse carts." But by 1840, another resident Corine Edwards described Newnansville as a fine city of logs. The Summerlin home was in a particularly dangerous location and, in early 1836, Summerlin moved part of his family at Newnansville and his wife went to Jefferson County.[7]

Although Newnansville provided a safe harbor for hundreds of refugees, perhaps as many as 1,000 by 1838, Indians from a large camp located in a nearby hammock made periodic attacks on Fort Gilleland and Newnansville. The Newnansville militia had its first major encounter with the Indians in September 1836 at San Felasco Hammock, a stand of large hardwood trees. Lieutenant Colonel W.J. Mills of the Sixth Florida later stated that all the companies at Newnansville saw action on that day; so it is almost certain that Summerlin and his sons Jake, Joseph and John, two of whom were only in their teens, participated in what turned out to be a two hour battle.

Colonel John Warren, who was out on a reconnaissance patrol when approximately 300 Seminole warriors pounced on his column, commanded a militia unit of "25 gentlemen citizens, 100 mounted volunteers and 25 U.S. troops." The militia retreated into the San Felasco Hammock and set up a perimeter. Warren had a cannon, which determined the outcome of the battle. The Seminoles launched two attacks, but the fire of the cannon eventually stemmed their attacks and they withdrew.[8]

Even with the threat that faced Newnansville, the settlement became a boomtown with all the associated problems of poor sanitation, overcrowding, deplorable housing, a lack of food and contagious diseases, drunkenness and even gun fights. Families at Newnansville lived on short rations and, according to D.B. McKay in *Florida Pioneers*, in 1836 the senior Summerlin left Newnansville with his sons, Jake and John, to salvage food from their deserted homestead some thirty-five miles away.

It was near dusk before they reached the Alligator area and were surprised to find that most of the buildings were intact, along with stores of sweet potatoes,

---

[6]Jacob R. Motte. *Journey Into Wilderness*. Reprint. (Gainesville: University of Florida Press, 1963), p. 89-90.

[7]Mary Burnett Papers, owned by author, 1835-1836.

[8]Mahon, *History of the Second Seminole War*, p. 179.

corn meal, and even bacon. After loading up their wagon, they stopped for a short rest before returning to Fort Gilleland when the trio was suddenly alerted by the sound of a sheep bell—a sound that probably saved their lives. They guessed, correctly it turned out, that the "sheep leader" had been disturbed by a Seminole war party. As they frantically made preparations to leave, the sheep suddenly stampeded toward the house. In seconds they were on their ponies and away, their wagon hauling a full load of supplies. They could hear the cutting sound of *minie* balls through the pines and the familiar and frightening war cry, "Yo-ho-echee," of the Seminole warriors. According to Mary Ida Bass Barber Shearhart in *Florida's Frontier, The Way Hit Wuz*, "It was a frightful, screeching, blood curdling cry."[9] When they stopped for a moment to let their ponies rest, they could see an eerie red glow lighting up the horizon where their homestead was burning. But they eventually managed to return to Newnansville, unharmed and with most of their load.[10]

Florida's early territorial militia was competent, but it would get better, and soon. In 1829, Achille Murat, a lieutenant colonel of the Florida militia and nephew of Napoleon Bonaparte, noted that these Florida volunteers "are inured to all fatigues and privations of almost savage life of the first settlement [with] their abundance of frontier skills and [despite] their less than reassuring appearance." And, he added, "Each man had his favorite horse and trusty carbine." These soldiers were canny woodsmen and could find their way by the sun and tree bark. They wore homespun clothes, twisted palm leaf hats and carried supplies for themselves and their horses tied behind the saddle. While they lacked much in appearance, they were excellent soldiers.

While still in his teens, in 1836, Jake, along with his brother, John, joined Captain James Edwards' Company of the First Regiment, Second Brigade of the Florida Mounted volunteers. They enrolled at Fort Bleckham, and each brought with him a horse and a firearm, which was customary with the Florida militiamen at that time. Some soldiers, however, would bring more than one horse, particularly if they were enlisting for more than three months. Often militiamen like Summerlin had better firearms than Army regulars.[11]

The Summerlins were a part of the so-called "volunteer militia companies which were included as organized parts of their respective geographically designated brigades." Some members, such as Jacob Summerlin had previous military training or experience, but many did not. "Drills, for instance, were not

---

[9]Mary Ida Bass Barber Shearhart, *Florida's Frontier, The Way It Wuz.* (Cocoa: The Florida Historical Society Press, 2004), p. 7.

[10]An Occasional Correspondent of the Tribune, "King of the Crackers," New York *Daily Tribune*, 16 Sept. 1883, p. 9.

[11]Jacob Summerlin and John Summerlin, Muster Rolls, Florida Mounted Militia, 1839-1840; Applications for Pensions During Florida Indian Wars, National Archives, Washington, DC.

generally mandatory." Referring to these local militia units in *Florida's Army*, Robert Hawk described them as "a mixed bag of potential soldiers with a wide range of military competence, and formal drill training, they fought well when the true test of combat came."[12] Time would show that this was especially true of young Jake as he would later prove on numerous scouting missions over much of the state for both military and civilian expeditions.[13]

Florida Governor Richard Call was dismayed over the conditions in Columbia County, but as territorial governor, he had no jurisdiction over the regular army—only the militia. He had no authority from the federal government to pay for the territory's defense or to provide assistance to settlers. Some help—in the way of corn—was sent to Fort White and distributed to citizens in Alachua and Columbia County, but protection from the Indians was still left up to local volunteer militia companies. None of the Summerlin men nor others who served in the Columbia County militia were ever paid for their services, but most men who served, as well as their widows, would later be declared eligible for federal pensions

In 1837, during a brief lull in hostilities, the Summerlins, along with other settlers in the Alligator area, returned to their homesteads to rebuild and replant. The Seminoles were also planting and harvesting crops in preparation for further warfare. After General Zachary Taylor won a costly victory against several hundred warriors near Lake Okeechobee on Christmas day, many whites felt the Indian threat was coming to an end. "But for the people of Columbia County and adjacent areas, it was only a new phase." Guerilla warfare by the Seminoles became more prevalent, and isolated homesteads were regularly attacked. It was an effective tactic by the Seminoles who seemed to be everywhere at once and who would retreat into the Okefenokee Swamp to the north or other jungle areas, such as the San Pedro Swamp or the Weteemka Hammocks to the south and east.[14] On December 20, 1837, Jake volunteered for militia service once again. This time he enrolled in Captain Livingston's newly created company at Fort Palmetto, which was attached to Colonel Warren's 6th Regiment of the Florida Mounted Volunteers. During his tour with this unit, he served as a scout.

Summerlin's enlistment expired on June 5, 1838, but on June 15, he signed up with Captain George W. Smith's company attached to the Second Regiment of the 6th Florida Mounted Volunteers, which was stationed at Mineral Springs near the confluence of the Suwannee and Withlachoochee Rivers. Most of the

---

[12]Robert Hawk, *Florida's Army, Militia, State Troops and National Guard: 1565 – 1985.* (Sarasota: Pineapple Press, 1986), pp. 54-55.

[13]Jacob Summerlin, *Ibid.*

[14]Mahon, *History of the Second Seminole War*, pp. 246, 248, 253; Keuchel, *History of Columbia County*, p. 44, 56-58.

militia units operating in this part of Florida were used for patrol duty and for the protection of local settlers, and few enlistments lasted over three months. While there were sometimes sharp firefights between the Indians and the militia, the Seminoles usually fought in small, swift moving bands—attacking, ambushing and then quickly vanishing.[15]

By 1839, courts in Columbia County had not met for three years because of Indian hostilities. This created some unusual problems. Typical was that of a man named John Bryan, whose wife had run away with another man and "was living in adultery." He could not legally obtain a divorce and remarry until the courts could hear his case, but eventually, the state legislation granted him a divorce by an enactment on February 14, 1840.[16] On November 5, 1839, Jake and his brother, John, signed on with Captain J. Edward Tucker's newly formed company. He gave his age as 19 years and his occupation as cattleman. Under Tucker, Jake and his brother probably rode more, saw more and fought more than anytime during the war.

Tucker's company was first sent to Fort Taylor, located on the west side of Lake Winder, about 130 miles south of Newnansville. The Fort was located on a mound surrounded by a plane of saw grass, interspersed with stands of pine and cypress. Describing his assignment at Fort Taylor, a U.S. Army Surgeon named Forry wrote, "Our position here is indeed melancholy. After each rain we resemble Noah on the top of Mount Ararat. Clouds of crows and black birds then hover around, waiting for the water to subside, to resume their daily vocation of picking corn. Turning young eye to the earth you then behold a score of glandered and sore backed mules! Now a mosquito buzzes in your ear, and next a flea bites you between the shoulders."[17]

At other times there were droughts when troops had to drink stagnant water. Rattlesnakes and moccasins were found everywhere on the peninsula, but oddly enough, no soldiers were ever reported as having died from snakebites. The soldiers were constantly tortured from the heat, cypress knees, saw grass, thick underbrush, poison oak, and thorny ti-ti vines. General Thomas Sidney Jessup described serving in Florida as the worst duty in the country. Before the war ended, more men died from diseases than from Seminole weapons.

In their rugged southward ride, Tucker's men saw plenty of Indian signs and were attacked by a party of Mikasuki braves close to Fort Taylor. On their return journey to Newnansville, the company was fired upon and took casualties at Fort Macomb, again at Fort Crane (probably Drane) and at Fort Wheeler,

---

[15]Muster Rolls, Old Military Records, National Archives, Washington, DC.

[16]Mahon, *History of the Second Seminole War*, p. 273; Keuchel, *History of Columbia County*, p. 53.

[17]Mahon, *History of the Second Seminole War*, p. 240.

but neither Jake nor John received a scratch.[18]

This long, painstaking expedition was spent trying to locate Indian encampments; unlike the duty they were normally engaged in, which had been to patrol the areas around their homesteads, to protect their own farms and to respond immediately to Indian attacks. Through his service with Tucker, Summerlin got a glimpse of a part of the Florida frontier that later in life he would ride over many times while driving or hunting wild cattle. Tucker's company was mustered out on January 31, 1840, but by November 1840, Jake, along with his father, enlisted again—this time in George McLellan's Company of the Second Regiment of the Mounted Florida Volunteers, a part of the brigade commanded by Colonel F. Dancy. That year the federal government appropriated $1,000,000 for military expenditures for the pacification of Indians in East Florida. McLellan's company patrolled the area between Newnansville and Alligator. It remained active until November 28, 1841.[19]

It was not at all unusual for militia volunteers, like the Summerlins, to serve in several companies. Some companies would sometime muster out after only three or six months and volunteers would return to their families to "help out." Most enlistees were yeoman farmers and would even return to their homestead to try to plant or harvest a crop during the intermittent periods of war and peace. George Cassel described this informal practice in his dissertation, "*In Defense of Florida:*" *The Organized Florida Militia From 1821 to 1920*,[20] "there were numerous comings and goings to and from the seat of war by the settlers." It was, of course, a custom that began early in American military history when there were extended campaigns against Native Americans or European powers in North America. The inability of George Washington to keep militia units in the field beyond a few months was one of his chief vexations, but the seasonal character of farming placed an added responsibility on these citizen soldiers who had to feed their families.

The Army regulars stationed in Florida frequently criticized the Florida militia, and the militia had little of a positive nature to say about the regulars. The army commander, General Jessup, was particularly critical of the militia volun-

---

[18]Reports of military activities of Captain J.A. Stewart, Florida Mounted Militia Co., Captain J.E. Tucker, Florida Mounted Militia Co., Captain McClellan, Florida Mounted Militia Co. and Captain James Livingston's Florida Mounted Militia Co. Jacob Summerlin, Junior, served in all companies at various times from Dec. 20, 1836 to April 1, 1841. National Archives, Record and Pension Office, Washington, DC: 17 Jan 1894.

[19]*Ibid.*

[20]George Cassel Bittle, *In Defense of Florida: The Organized Florida Militia From 1821-1920*, Dissertation at Florida State University, 1954; U.S. Congress, *House Document*, 78; "Compiled Service Records of Volunteer Soldiers Who Served in Organizations from State of Florida, 1835-1858." *Florida Wars, Pension Records.* R.G. 1025, S608 – Roll 30, Florida State Archives, Tallahassee.

teers after they proved reluctant when he wanted to employ them during the summer, the so-called "sickly season," when soldiers normally suspended campaigning. However, one soldier of the Second U.S. Dragoons described the Florida volunteers as being equal to the regulars in every way on scouting missions and added that Florida men comprised the best volunteer force in the Territory.[21]

Military strategies constantly changed as new commanders were given control of the war that was becoming more-and-more expensive in terms of lives and property. The war had become very unpopular with many Americans because Americans had traditionally been opposed to prolonged wars. Secretary of War Joel Poinsett, who had earlier divided the militia and regulars into separate commands, ordered a strategy of "an incessant scout, attack and pursuit." [22] Jake Summerlin was assigned to Colonel William S. Harney's command in central Florida, and according to Albert Devane, was given credit for discovering a large Seminole encampment on Hilliards' Island near present day Kissimmee. Following the discovery, Harney's soldiers quickly attacked the camp, but most of the Seminoles escaped, although they left behind several hundred head of cattle.[23]

By the summer of 1841, settlers began to move back into parts of Columbia County after a company of mounted militia occupied Fort White. By the spring of 1842, 651 people, including men, women, children and slaves, had drifted back into twelve resettlement areas between Fort Gilleland and Fort White.[24] Tragically this resettlement "again triggered a resumption of Indian raids." In this year, settlers in Columbia County experienced some of the worst atrocities of the war. One of the reasons that the Indians in east Florida became more aggressive was due to the fact that by the last of March 1841, all citizen soldiers in Florida were discharged. This, of course, included all of Colonel John Warren's regiment to which the Summerlins had been attached during most of their service. Protection for the settlers was left up to the Army regulars, some 5,000 men, who had to defend the entire Florida Territory. President William Henry Harrison, famed for his triumphs at the Battles of Tippecanoe and the Thames River with militia units, might have expected more of the militia on duty in Florida. But according to John K. Mahon, "One of the main reasons was cost." According to the U.S. Paymaster General, "It cost more to field citizen soldiers than regulars." Floridians opposed the shift and clamored for a renewed use of

---

[21]Mahon, *History of the Second Seminole War*, pp. 208-210, 241-242, 256, 290; Hawk, *Florida's Army*, pp. 59-67.

[22]Mahon, *History of the Second Seminole War*, p. 208; Joe Knetsch, *Florida's Seminole Wars, 1817-1858.* (Charleston, SC: Arcadia Publishing, 2003), pp. 125-126.

[23]Albert Devane, *Early Florida History.* (Sebring Historical Soc., 1978).

[24]Keuchel, *History of Columbia County*, pp. 148-150; Mahon, p. 301.

citizen soldiers. Richard Call described the area of middle and east Florida as, "an entire wilderness of which Indians have possession."[25] A band of Creeks under the leadership of Chief Halpatter Tustenuggee terrorized the whole area in and around Columbia County. One of the most vicious attacks was carried out against members of the Tillis family near Newnansville. "On February 24, 1842, Mrs. Tillis was shot down in the yard while a young lady staying with her was stabbed twice by a butcher knife." Arrows were shot into five of the Tillis children. An arrow went all the way through one child who still lived for twenty-four hours. After this carnage, the Seminoles plundered the house before vanishing into the woods to escape soldiers sent out from Fort White. An army surgeon, who arrived with other soldiers from Fort White, encountered this grisly scene and, working desperately, managed to save the lives of two of the victims.[26]

Seminole war parties attacked several other families in Columbia County, and on May 14 and 15, 1842, a small band led by Octahachee struck Alligator and the surrounding area killing four more civilians. This was the last major disturbance in Columbia County during the long war, but as John K. Mahon wrote in *History of the Second Seminole War*, "the war did not come to an abrupt end, but rather dragged itself out."[27]

In 1842, Summerlin was in his early twenties and he had already spent nearly half of his life as a soldier in a protracted Indian war, and it would not be the last war in which he would be involved.

The prolonged conflict had been a tragedy in many ways. Besides the loss of lives, damage to property was widespread. The cost to the government for prosecuting the war was estimated at over forty million dollars. The long war had also weakened territorial banks, deepened the depression of 1837 and delayed statehood. The Seminole nation had all but been destroyed and its remnants scattered from the depths of the Everglades to the Oklahoma Territory.[28] If anything can be considered positive about the war, it was the creation of military roads into the interior and the enactment of the Armed Occupation Act of 1842, which opened millions of acres of land to settlement in Central and South Florida. The Act provided the inducement for Jake, his in-laws and many other intrepid pioneers to settle in the wildest parts of Florida.

Immediately after the hostilities, Jake and the rest of his family remained in

---

[25]Knetsch, *Florida's Seminole Wars*, p. 93; Mahon, *History of the Second Seminole War*, pp. 292-293.

[26]Keuchel, *History of Columbia County*, pp. 56-57; *Niles Register*, LXII, 9 April 1842, p. 85.

[27]Mahon, *History of the Second Seminole War*, p. 320.

[28]Keuchel, *History of Columbia County*, p. 58; James W. Covington, *The Seminoles of Florida*. (Gainesville: University Press of Florida, p. 199), p. 109; Knetsch, *Florida's Seminole Wars*, p. 141; Tebeau, p. 168.

northern Columbia County and returned to farming. There were no war casualties in the immediate Summerlin family, although Jake's mother had died in 1836. Her death, however, was not related to the long war, and she probably died of scarlet fever or tuberculosis. Jake's father married a widow, Elizabeth Jones, during the war, and the Summerlin family expanded as Jake acquired new "step" and "half" siblings.

The expansion of cotton production ushered a new period of economic growth and development in Columbia County following the war. The economic uncertainties of the late 1830s came to a close as the textile mills of Great Britain and New England again clamored for southern cotton.[29] A population explosion accompanied the economic growth and soon Florida experienced an onslaught of thousands of new settlers.

Jake became more interested in cattle production during the years following the end of the war, and he was ready to move to an area that offered unlimited rangeland, where property could be homesteaded under the Armed Occupation Act of 1842 and, as one writer observed, "one could ride days and never tire of seeing the pure wonders of a land as God created it, a land totally unsettled."[30]

Jake matured into a strikingly handsome man. Information from enlistment rolls indicated that he was five foot eight or ten inches tall — about average height for a male at the time. He carried himself erect and gave the impression of being taller. His facial features were described as being rather heroic with a broad forehead and a face dominated by calm self-assurance. He had brown hair, and his eyes were blue and penetrating. His expression was usually an earnest one with a thoughtful gaze. He liked to talk and laugh, but he would listen with total concentration. Reporters who met him later in life may have exaggerated his indomitable qualities, but what reporter has failed to varnish the truth a bit? As one reporter wrote, "there was a certain sense of destiny about his demeanor." Another would describe him later as "not a large man but a man of iron constitution and immense physical power, and a person who felt that he was born to use his powers and his energies to the fullest."[31]

He claimed that he had never taken a drop of spirits. This, along with his rugged honesty, rather amused and amazed the sea captains from Cuba who would later buy cattle from him. Most people in the Territory were aware of his reputation for honesty and straight dealing.

Jake always enjoyed company, but his real delight was the solitude of the outdoors when he was astride his favorite horse, *Morgan*. In many ways, he was

---

[29]Keuchel, *History of Columbia County*, pp. 59-60.

[30]Covington, *The Seminoles of Florida*, p. 110.

[31]Louise Frisbie, "Biography of Jacob Summerlin," *The Polk County Democrat*, 3 December 1973; Bartow *Informant*, 27 Jan. 1883.

introspective — more interested in ideas than things. While not very literate, his interest in ideas qualified him as an intellectual. In time he would become rich, respected, even revered, but he still showed a love for the simple things in life. His clothing was always rustic and he was rarely seen wearing a dress coat or suit. Summerlin never felt he had to prove himself to others. As far as is known, he was never in any kind of frontier shootout, yet he was an excellent shot.[32]

He derived great pleasure from his large family, his many friends, his success in solving problems and his acts of benevolence. Although he was held in the highest respect by many of his peers, he seemed almost reluctant to command. He was always a private during the Indian wars. Later, however, he commanded a mounted company for a short time during the Civil War, but throughout his life, he seemed uncomfortable in positions of leadership. He empathized with the poor and destitute, particularly orphans or widows. He had a keen sense of justice. When he thought that a certain large cattle owner had altered the brand on one of his cows, he took him to court, using the law to protect his property, instead of relying on harsher forms of frontier justice. Nevertheless, property for ownership's sake meant little to him and he was always willing to help anyone out who was destitute and often gave them cattle.[33]

Jake survived the dangers of the Second Seminole War, but in 1844, he fell victim to the charms of a comely and graceful twenty-year-old widow named Frances Knight Zipperer, the daughter of Samuel and Mary Roberts Knight, a prominent family from Glynn and Lowndes County, Georgia. Frances' late husband, John Jacob Zipperer, had died at Fort Crane during the war, leaving her with one child, Gideon. Nothing is known of their courtship, but Frances and Jake married at Newnansville in Alachua County on February 13, 1845, the same year that Florida became a state. Their marriage would be a prosperous and successful one. Jake immediately adopted Frances' son, Gideon, who would become an integral part of the Summerlin household and Jake's cattle business.[34]

He voted in Florida's first statewide election on May 26, 1845, at Alligator. Richard Keith Call ran on a Whig ticket, but was defeated in the general election by William D. Moseley, a Democrat and a Jefferson County planter. Because Jake's father was a close friend of Call's and an avid Whig, it is presumed he voted for Call who had already served as territorial governor two times. The 1845 election turned out to be a bitter contest of personalities and Call was accused of deserting the Democratic Party to improve his political and financial fortunes. Since the Democrats were the party of statehood, they carried the election.[35]

---

[32]*Ibid.*

[33]*Ibid.*

[34]*Ibid.*

[35]Tebeau, *A History of Florida*, pp. 171-176.

Jake and Sam Summerlin coordinated with William Towles in 1876 to build a twenty-mile fence from near LaBelle to the Okaloacoochee Slough to keep their cattle from straying into the Everglades. It was later named the Summerlin-Towles-Lucky Fence. Sam Lucky actually supervised the construction of the fence. (Illustration by Joe Akerman)

Chapter 3

Pioneers of the Palmetto Prairies

Except when the moon shines very brightly, a fire is a necessary protection against wild animals. Even the cattle understand this and are less easily frightened when in site of the fire.
Rev. S.A.W. Jewett, *Livingston in Africa*, 1868

As the frontier inched westward in most of the country during the 1840s, in Florida it generally moved southward. Except for a few coastal towns, in the 1840s the interior of the territory south of Newnansville was almost completely undeveloped—almost devoid of white settlers. Most of the few remaining Native Americans had taken refuge in the Everglades. However, they still remained an occasional threat to isolated ranchers, farmers or trading posts.

In 1843, Samuel Knight, Jake's father-in-law, became one of the first pioneers to establish an agricultural operation in what is now Hillsborough County. He also served as South Florida's first Methodist preacher during the 1840s. Under the 1842 Armed Occupation Act, Florida lands became available for homesteading and Knight moved his rather large family from Lowndes County Georgia, to a homestead near present day Plant City. Knight was a veteran of the war and was familiar with the geography of this area. After the war, he had made a more careful exploration of the territory with two of his sons-in-law, George Hamilton and John Zipperer. It was a land beautiful in its primeval naturalness with plenty of grass for raising cattle. There was also an abundance of game and herds of wild cattle, descended mostly from Andulusian-Spanish stock.[1]

Jake, his new wife and a brother-in-law, Frank Varn, drove a herd of cracker cattle from South Georgia and Columbia County to the wilderness site Samuel Knight had named Knight's Station. Jake turned his herd out on "a part of that

---

[1]Kyle VanLandingham and Joe Akerman, "Florida's Early Cattle Kings," unpublished manuscript.

vast stretch of expectant acreage...on the Spanish borderlands."[2] His cattle mixed with the native cattle already there, becoming as wild as buffalo. It was a heroic saga that was played out many times on America's frontier during the nineteenth century. According to Frank L. Owsley, this method of migration and settlement was typical for rich and poor on the southern frontier, "Friends and relatives living in the same neighboring communities formed one or more parties and moved out together, and when they had reached the promised land, they constituted a new community, which was called a 'settlement' — and still is so called." The settlements were often miles apart, and even the inhabitants of a single settlement might be broadly scattered. "After the first trek," other settlers, usually relatives or friends, might come "filling in the interstices."[3]

Soon after, Jake, Frances, or "Fannie," and Gideon settled about four miles south of Knight's Station at a deserted Indian camp named Itchepuckesassa, "they began housekeeping in the piney woods with Frances cooking their meals in the open woods while Jake cut down trees with which to build a home. A rude shelter of poles and brush were hastily erected where household furniture was stored beneath until a log house could be built."[4]

Simply staying alive on the Florida frontier was a tremendous task. However, deer, turkey and wild hogs were plentiful and the lakes, streams and rivers were full of fish. Of course, surviving was more difficult for some than it was for Jake and Fannie. Both were experienced with the demands of the frontier marches where the common denominator for survival and success in this cattleman's Canaan was labor — hard and always increasing physical labor. Lessons learned by Abraham and the children of Israel over 4,000 years ago were applied here in much the same form. For years they would give the land their labor, their devotion and their love and, like all successful frontiersmen, they gave under conditions of great physical stress and times of loneliness, isolation, and difficulty. Their personalities were strongly endowed with the work ethic and not the least of their many virtues that helped them survive was a deep reservoir of patience.

This love for the land that the Summerlins and the Knights shared became a lasting bond between the modern Florida cattleman and these pioneer stockmen. That ethos can be summarized in a few words, "Land should be utilized for the production of food." An eighty-year-old ranch widow, who lived in Central Florida only twenty miles from Disney World, summed up this tradi-

---

[2]Lillie McDuffie, *The Lures of Manatee* (Brackeston: 1961), p. 196; Doyle Conner, "The History of the Florida Cattle Industry," *Florida Cattle Frontier* (Kissimmee: Florida Cattlemen's Association and Florida Cracker Cattle Breeder's Association, 1995), p. 5; *Ibid.*, pp. 11-12.

[3]Frank Owsley L., *Plain Folk of the Old South* (Baton Rouge: Louisiana State University Press, 1949), p. 62.

[4]VanLandingham and Akerman, "Florida's Early Cattle Kings," p. 28.

tion to me a few years ago in a single sentence. She did not consider herself and her family wealthy, although "It is true we own sixty-five thousand acres of land, but that land is for raising cattle—not to be sold or exploited in any way."[5]

A visitor once described this part of Florida as "a trackless waste of open prairies, scrub palmettos, pines and scattered hammocks." But it was a more complex ecological system than this. A great deal of it was made up of pine flatwoods with sandy soils on an underlying hardpan. The relief is generally low, although large sections are marked by sandy ridges covered with long leaf pines and turkey oaks. Along the rivers' flood plains and near the bay heads, the native grass was often rich. Maiden cane grew in great abundance. However, during the rainy summers, the shallow underlying hardpan often hindered drainage and caused serious flooding. During the dry winters, the flatwoods became susceptible to fire—some caused by lightning. The periodic floods, which usually deposited silt and vegetable debris, provided some of the best soil and grasses for grazing livestock. During cow hunts, both heretics (unbranded cows) and branded cattle were often found in these areas and in the river hammocks. Cattle were naturally drawn to the best forage, but when good forage was not available, these cracker cattle could survive on very little. Preconditioned in Spain and Florida by centuries of environmental extremes and by selective breeding in Spain, they were the hardiest of the European breeds brought to Florida. "While other breeds vanished, the Spanish foundlings survived." Blood serum tests made from modern cracker cattle have demonstrated that ninety-five percent of their genetic makeup is the same as that of Spanish breeds in Andalusia.[6]

Although most of the land that surrounded the Summerlin and Knight homesteads was referred to as "third rate" by early explorers and surveyors, there was plenty of it—enough to support large, widely dispersed, herds. It was estimated that at least twenty acres of flatwoods were required to support one cow. Some of the cattle that were branded by Summerlin and the Knights literally ranged over thousands of acres. Hunting or rounding them up for branding and cropping, penning, and driving to markets usually took at least four to five months.[7]

One of the main staples of pioneer families' diets was a rich flour or starch processed from the wild coontie plant [*Zania floridana*]. Native Americans used it for generations, and the early settlers learned the technique from them. It

---

[5]Mrs. Henry Partin, rancher and wife of Henry Partin, rancher. Personal Interview, Kissimmee, 5 May 1975.

[6]Joe Akerman, *Florida Cowman*, pp. 12, 13, 264, 265; George H. Dacy, *Four Centuries of Florida Cattle Raising.* (St. Louis: 1948), pp. 11, 22.

[7]Mrs. Berta Chaires, Cattlewoman in Dixie County, Personal Interview, Old Town, Fla: 15 May 1975; Akerman, *Florida Cowman*, pp. 160-162.

grew in abundance in most of Florida. Used primarily to make bread, pioneer cooks found that tasty custards also could be made from the starch by sweetening it with honey, sugar or homemade syrup. Other substitutes for staples were found. As Myrtle Hilliard Crow points out in *Old Tales and Trails of Florida*, pioneers like Summerlin learned to make a salt substitute from black jack oak, "It was cut green and burned. The next morning before the dew dried, a thin crust was scraped off [the branch] during the night."[8]

The few settlers around Itchepuckesassa and Knights' Station, including the Summerlins, used the "Indian way" of grinding corn, meal and grits by using rocks and stones. But the resourceful Jake Summerlin purchased a gristmill in St. Augustine and had it shipped to Tampa Bay from where it was hauled overland to Knights' Station. Once the mill was set up, Jake designated every Friday or Saturday as "mill day or grinding day." Grinding was usually done on a toll basis, and, as was so often true of the frontier, no money was charged for the grinding.[9]

Boots and shoes were often homemade from home tanned cowhides, which were either cured by stretching or by using lime and tannic acid. The lime was used to remove the hair from the skins, and the hides were prepared or tanned in tannic acid.

Although the region around Knights' Station was not cotton country, Jake and most other settlers had small cotton patches. The harvested cotton was converted into a rough cloth known as osnaburg. The final product was generally white or light colored, but for variety it was sometimes dyed with wild indigo, which turned the material into a blue-black shade. Finer woven material known as muslin could be smoothed out and was sometimes used for underwear; however, finer grades of cloth were usually purchased from dry goods stores. One of Jake's sons, Samuel Summerlin, would later recall seeing his mother, Frances, carding cotton—a tiresome but necessary part of the process. He also remembered seeing his sister, Martha, spin it.[10]

The Summerlins and other nearby settlers were often concerned about small bands of Seminoles and Mikasukis who sometimes wandered from the reservation, presumably in search of cattle. Game such as deer, evidently became scarce after more white settlers came into the interior and the Indians were forced to look for food beyond the reservation. This search for food was a common cause for conflict wherever there was frontier expansion in America. Summerlin would later point out that this problem became especially bad with the invention of the Winchester rifle, which held fourteen rounds. He said that he had seen as many as seven deer killed at one time "for the mere purpose of test-

---

[8]Crow, *Tales and Trails*, 50.
[9]"Uncle Crews Recalls Events of Bartow Pioneers," *Polk County Record*, 18 Aug. 1932.
[10]*Ibid.*

ing these rifles." A Seminole told Summerlin, "White man comes, he brings cold on the Indians' head and hunger to his belly."[11]

One of the main problems the Summerlins faced in trying to establish a sizeable foundation herd of cattle was the great number of predators that roamed the woods. There was no real pressure on the population of animals in the area where the Summerlins lived and, although Native Americans might occasionally kill a bear or a panther, these predatory animals were generally left alone. Besides black bears and panthers, the woods in this part of Florida were also full of red wolves. Newborn livestock were particularly vulnerable to all of these animals, and panthers and wolves would even attack full-grown cattle. Occasionally, wild predators would attack humans.

There was a well-known account of an actor who was visiting Florida on tour in the early 1800s. He was separated from his touring group somehow and, when his remains were found, it was determined that he had been killed and eaten by a pack of wolves. On another occasion, a panther viciously attacked Bronson Lewis, a cattleman. Although he was able to club the panther to death and escape, he was crippled for the rest of his life.

A much less tragic panther encounter occurred when Jake and his son, Sam, were hunting cattle near old Fort Cummings. One evening after they had turned in to sleep, they were awakened by the frightful screams of two panthers that were fighting. Jake grabbed a lightwood knot from their campfire and threw it in the direction of the big cats. They both scampered off into a nearby swamp and were not heard from again.[12]

A much smaller predator, but one that could be lethal to both man and beast, was the Florida mosquito. They often appeared in blinding swarms and could bring a cow or horse down or strike a person with malaria or yellow jack. When George Franklin Thompson of the Freedman's Bureau toured Central Florida and the lower west coast of Florida in 1866, he described the staggering number of mosquitoes along the Peace River:

> At dusk [we] cast anchor near an island about seven miles from the mouth of Peace Creek. Here we were attacked by Musquitoes [sic] at first by brigades then by divisions and afterwards by corps, and doubting our ability to withstand their severe charges, we concluded it would be wiser to retreat. Consequently, we fell back about two miles and passed a miserable night in the boat.[13]

---

[11]Crow, *Tales and Trails*, p. 56.

[12]*Ibid.*, p. 56.

[13]George Franklin Thompson, U.S. Freedman's Bureau, Refugees and Abandoned Lands, On Tour of Central Florida. Box #24, P.K. Yonge Library, Gainesville: 1865-1866, p. 85.

Florida's unpredictable and often violent weather proved as dangerous as predators to cattlemen. High winds frequently roared across the palmetto prairies accompanied by torrential rains and explosive lightening. Myrtle Hilliard Crow described the devastations of the monsoon-like rains that swept down the Kissimmee Valley, an area where the Summerlins ran cattle, in early summer:

> The Tohopekaligas, Cypress, Hatchenaha and Kissimmee Lakes were like one huge lake ... and the starving cattle floated down the Kissimmee River, eating cabbage palmettos, fiber and stems, grasses, sprouts, maiden cane, tree limbs, moss, etc. Near Fort Gardner on the west side of the Kissimmee River between Lake Hatchenaha and Lake Kissimmee ... cattlemen watched bunches of fifty to sixty head of cattle passing there and landing in the vicinity of Camp Hammock.[14]

Jake once lost several hundred head of cattle near the Hillsborough River during a hurricane. Most drowned, but others were killed by falling trees and flying debris.

During the years while Summerlin worked to establish a sizeable cattle herd and to make contacts with buyers, he was compelled to take on a variety of not-so-profitable pursuits. His dry goods operation was by far the most lucrative, but he also served for a short time as a deputy sheriff in Hillsborough County for another cattleman, John Parker. In 1846, a time when there were few roads other than the military and Indian trails, he was appointed a road commissioner for the Third District of Hillsborough County.[15]

Perhaps the most important road in the entire county was a neglected military road running from Fort Brooke near Tampa Bay to Fort Mellon, part of present day Sanford. The road had been important during the Second Seminole War because it connected with the Fort King—Fort Brook Road south of the Hillsborough River. After the war, however, both roads deteriorated into little more than stretches of grown-over clearings, sometimes nothing more than "cut out" trails, which were frequently under water and full of pot holes and stumps. But they were important to the few settlers who used them. Summerlin, who was aware of the importance of improving transportation in the interior, was unable to accomplish much. There was always a lack of funds and many Floridians still considered waterways as the best way to accommodate the transportation needs of an expanding population.[16]

In 1830, Congress appropriated $10,400 to study the possibility of establishing a cross-state waterway and, sometime between 1845 and 1847, Jake was asked

---

[14]Crow, *Osceola Sun*, Date missing.

[15]"Florida Reminisces," *The Florida Sun*, 16 Sept. 1876.

[16]*Ibid.*

to lead a survey party across the state to find the best possible route for such a canal. His reputation as a scout and his decisive and dependable character had been firmly established during the Indian Wars and because of this, it was logical that he was called upon for this task. His father had worked as a surveyor and had taught him some of the required skills. A party made up of Captain M.L. Smith, Lieutenant W.F. "Baldy" Smith and Lieutenant Bryan met Summerlin at Mellonville on the St. Johns River. From there, he led them on what he thought could be a possible watercourse. Captain Smith later wrote about Summerlin's "eminent fitness for such a position:"

> Some short time after the survey was begun and after crossing the Palatlakala Creek... in passing over some flat woods of pine and palmetto growth, Summerlin suddenly stopped and pointing to a pine said, "I killed a deer at the root of that pine last year." I looked surprised from the fact of there being no road or path or anything to distinguish one pine from another, and he [Jake] said to me, "you don't believe me?" [We] went to the tree, and there, sure enough, was the remains of the skeleton of a deer. Mr. Summerlin did not subsequently command an army, but from his immense herd of cattle he helped very greatly to feed them. This gentleman is now one of the largest stock owners in the state.[17]

On November 5, 1849, Summerlin was appointed postmaster of the tiny settlement of Hitchepucksassa (also spelled Itchepucksassa). Hitchepucksassa, originally called Fort Hitchepucksassa or Fort Sullivan, was located about four miles northeast of the site where Plant City would later be platted, near a deserted village by the same name. Fort Hitchepucksassa was originally built in 1839 at the height of the Second Seminole War. The spelling was later changed to Itchepuckesassa, and various other spellings are found in military communiqués and on different maps. Theodore Leslie pointed out that it had the peculiar distinction of never being spelled in the same manner twice.[18]

Hitchepucksassa was originally an Indian name, which had various meanings. The most accepted translation was "tobacco fields," but other interpretations were "many pipes" and "The place where the moon plants the colors of the rainbow, and the sun draws them out in the flowers." Summerlin was given credit for founding this settlement, which would later be given a more manageable name, "Cork." No more than a trading post owned by Summerlin, it became a gathering and trading point for cowmen and Indians. The 1850 Census listed only Ely and Vina Whitton, their two children, Piety and Laura,

---

[17]*Ibid.*

[18]"Summerlin Appointed Postmaster at Hitchepucksassa, Hillsborough County," U.S. Post Office Department Records of Appointments of Postmasters, 1832-1971. Florida State Archives, Tallahassee, M-841, Roll #20.

D.J. Boney, Peter Platt and Vina Whitton and, of course, the Summerlin family as residents of the Hitchepucksassa settlement. Some of these people lived many miles apart. For a short period in 1855, James D. Green replaced Summerlin as postmaster. A year later Summerlin succeeded Green and remained in that post for several more years.

Jake's trading post and post office was a sparse oasis on the Florida frontier that provided such pioneer necessities as plows, axes, guns, ammunition, saddles, blankets, clothes, seeds and other dry goods, which were usually hauled overland by oxen pulled trains from Fort Brooke.[19]

William C. Brown visited the Summerlin homestead in 1856 and made an interesting observation of Jake's wife, Fannie, and the people who lived in the general area:

> Frances, Summerlin's wife, is a rather pleasant woman....but they do not have many such women, extra ones in these parts....The people in this area look like and act like characters we read about in Cooper's (James Fennimore Cooper), Indian novels as near as I can judge.[20]

A gin for grinding corn and another for separating seed from cotton fiber were connected to Jake's post. "The cotton gin was similar to early cane grinding mills — where a horse or mule was hitched to a long pole and circled round and round turning the mechanism of the gin and separating the seeds from the fiber balls."[21]

As the number of Jake's enterprises grew, so did his family. In 1847 Fannie presented him with a daughter, Martha. Two years later, she bore a son, Jasper. And, in 1850, George was born. They would eventually have seven children including Jake's stepson, Gideon Zipperer. Always the family man, Summerlin loved them all and made sure that most had some formal education.

Not long after Jake and his family homesteaded in South Florida, he received word that his father had died. Jacob Summerlin had written his last will and testament on January 13, 1848, and two days later, he passed away at his home in Alligator. He was fifty-six. Jake's brother, John A. Summerlin, and two of his father's sons-in-law, Thomas D. Dexter and Robert Brooke, were listed as executors of the elder Summerlin's estate. The estate was sizable and included 500 acres of land, twenty-six slaves, $19,000 he had loaned for which he was drawing interest and 200 head of cattle. Sarah Pamela Williams referred to Jacob Summerlin in her reminis-

---

[19]U.S. Census, Hillsborough County, 1850; D.B. McKay, "Pioneer Florida," *Tampa Tribune,* 15 Nov. 1953, p. 1.

[20]William C. Brown, "Diary of Years From Dec. 24th, 1855, to April 9, 1856," February 19th 1856 at Summerlin Home at Ichepuckessa [*sic*].

[21]D.B. McKay, *Ibid.*

cences as "a rich old man." Other heirs to the estate included his third wife, Mary Ann Elizabeth Summerlin (maiden name probably Jones), and three of his daughters, Rebecca, Louise Ann and Caroline Victoria. He also specified that a ten-year-old slave girl named Fanny should be set at liberty at the age of twenty-one, "to act for herself with my wife Mary Ann Elizabeth Summerlin as her guardian."[22]

For some reason or through some oversight, Jake was not listed as an executor or even as a beneficiary in the publication of his father's assets that appeared in the paper after his death. A popular legend has been that Jake received several slaves from his father, which he sold and, with the money, bought cattle. Possibly Jacob had given these slaves to Jake just before he left for Hillsborough County. There is nothing to suggest that there was a rift between the two. Jake had returned to Alligator in 1845 and spent some time with his father. Near the time of the probation of the elder Summerlin's will, Jake bought fifty head of cattle from James Whitten of Ware County, Georgia. He later drove these cattle to Hillsborough County and they became part of his foundation herd.[23]

The obituary appearing in the Jacksonville News described the elder Summerlin "as a husband and parent, who was amiable and exemplary...and his unceremonious cordiality of manners and obliging disposition will long live in the community in which he resided." He was lauded for his service in both branches of the Florida Legislature and for his important service in the militia during "the contest between our government and the Seminole Indians."[24]

The Second Seminole War opened up a number of trails and crude roads in Hillsborough County, but for any successful and permanent development in the interior of the state, progressive Floridians knew that more and better roads were badly needed. In 1847, Jake was elected a magistrate of District Three in Hillsborough County. Part of his responsibility was to select sites for new roads. That year, he also served as a justice of the peace for the same district. During this time, he performed a number of marriages—one of which was between his sister-in-law, Mary Knight, and the famous Florida frontiersman and cattleman George Hamilton. As justice of the peace, one of his duties was also to certify cattle brands, which became a rather tricky but important task. Altering brands, a practice of dishonest cowmen, became more-and-more common as increasing numbers of settlers moved into Florida's interior. To further complicate matters, stock brands were issued by individual county governments and no central registration mechanism existed. Thus, the same "flank brand" might be issued by different counties. Ear crops and even the use of belly brands did help to simplify identification of livestock.[25]

---

[22]Jacob Summerlin, Senior, Copy of Last Will and Testament, 1 Jan. 1848 (copy owned by author); Denham and Brown, *Cracker Times*, p. 111.

[23]Denham and Brown, *Cracker Times*, p. 111.

[24]"Jacob Summerlin, Senior Obituary," Jacksonville News, 29 January 1848.

[25]Charles Lykes, Personal Interview, Tampa, FL, 2 May 1976.

Elder J.M. Hayman, a veteran of the Second Seminole War, was a delegate to the Florida Baptist State Convention organized at Concord, Madison, Florida in 1854. He was later employed by the Southern Baptist Association and pastured the Peas Creek Baptist Church in 1864. One year Hayman received only $4.50 for his ministry at this church.

Chapter 4

Further Unrest on the Florida Frontier

Although the Second Seminole War was technically over in 1842, and most of the Seminoles and Mikasukis had been transported to the West, small Indian hunting parties still roamed over parts of the state. They were frequently sighted in South and Central Florida. The Summerlin home was near a large hammock where Seminoles often camped. John O. Parrish wrote, "At no place in Florida could a location for a settlement have been chosen that have been better suited for an Indian attack...but for some reason there had been less devilment committed by Indians here than in other places...The great size of the hammock and its dense growth would easily have hidden a thousand Indians."[1] But by now there were only a few hundred Indians left in the central and southern part of Florida. Under General William J. Worth's Order #27, dated August 11, 1842, one group of Indians entered into a verbal agreement that they would live, plant, and hunt for present within the defined limits of a reservation. Worth tendered this as an official treaty to end the Second Seminole War. The territory referred to was established in 1839 and ran from "the mouth of Talakcchop or Pease Creek, up the left bank of that stream to the fork of the Southern branch, to the head, or northern edge of Lake Istakp, Georgia. Thence down the eastern margin of that lake to the stream which empties from it into the Kissimmee River, following the left bank of said stream and to where it empties into Lake Ockeechobee, south through said lake, and the Everglades to the Shark River, following the right bank to [the] Gulf, thence along [the] Gulf shore, to the place beginning, excluding all islands, lying between Punta Rassa and the head of Charlotte Harbor...."[2] Few settlers, especially those living on frontier, were happy with Worth's order because it made no allowance for transferring the remaining Indians to the West. Most settlers felt that the Army officers were too lenient with the Indians, and some settlers even advocated resuming hostilities with the few remaining Indians. One of the major prob-

---

[1] "Jacob Summerlin," *Courier Informant*, 11 July 1893.
[2] Knetsch, *Florida's Seminole Wars*, p. 142-143; Covington, *The Seminoles of Florida*, p. 108.

lems was that few people—both settlers and Native Americans—understood exactly where these boundaries were. A letter of October 15, 1845, addressed to Florida Governor William Moseley from Captain John Sprague, who was stationed with the Army at St. Augustine, drove this point home, "The Senate of the last Territorial Legislature of 1844, particularly those delegates from the Southern and Eastern sections, wanted no compromise and wanted Indians removed as opposed to views of Federal Government."[3]

Another letter to Moseley from Mayor Whiting at Fort Brooke, dated June 25, 1846, indicated that settlers in the Marion Springs and Palatka areas wanted protection from possible Indian attacks and asked for twenty-five to thirty muskets or rifles. Whiting wrote, "The excitement is great and unless men are placed upon the frontier, the whole country south to Tampa will be abandoned." Complaints by Army authorities were also lodged against the "aggression of whites upon the Indian Territory." But since there were no fences for cattle, cows often strayed onto reservation lands and cowmen entered the reservation to hunt them.

Jake, who had already spent a considerable part of his life scouting and fighting the Indians, sided with the other white settlers and felt that the only solution was to transfer the remaining Seminoles and Mikasukis to a western reservation. He was honest in his dealings with the Seminoles, which suggested that he understood the plight of Florida's Native Americans, but, at the same time, separation seemed the only viable solution to him and to most settlers.[4] It was the old Jacksonian conviction regarding Native Americans. As Joe Knetsch points out in *Florida's Seminole Wars, 1817-1858:*

> Immediately after the declaration of peace [1842], an attack took place in Hernando County that took the life of Mary Crum. Those responsible for her death had not been informed of the peace; however, the same could not be said for the attack on the house of Gideon Hague near San Falasco Hammock in Alachua County in June 1843...Early the following year another "outrage" took place west of the Apalachicola River and north of St. Andrews Bay.[5]

The new unrest became a political issue. "The Democrats, led by newly elected Senator David Levy Yulee, quickly attacked the official U.S. policy, and called for militia action." But the Whig leadership of the Army tended to argue

---

[3]Florida Governor William Moseley (Correspondence). Florida State Archives, Box 2, RG101, Series 679.

[4]*Ibid.*

[5]Knetsch, *Florida's Seminole Wars*, p. 144.

that the Democrats and Florida settlers were overreacting to this unrest.[6]

In July 1849, several Indians attacked a trading post located on the Peace River some sixty miles south of tiny Itchepuckesassa. During the same month, a small settlement on the Indian River near Fort Pierce was also attacked. Although the Army considered these attacks to be minor, members of the press at St. Augustine and Jacksonville reacted sharply and their outrage caused twenty-seven settlers to flee from the southeast coast to St. Augustine for protection.[7]

In 1850, a child belonging to the Sumner family of Okahumpka disappeared and it was assumed that the Seminoles had kidnapped him. James Covington, in a 1989 *Sunland Tribune* article, claimed the so-called "Sumner" boy was actually Dan Hubbard. The John Casey diary, however, claimed the boy had been killed by Ecko Ematkla Chopco in retaliation for a theft of some ponies by Jake Summerlin. Jake quickly organized a small posse of six riders. From Itchepuckesassa, the posse followed the signs of the suspected kidnappers into the deep reaches of the Withlacoochee basin. Summerlin later reported that after crossing a slough of mud and swamp, they entered an Indian village located on an island of some fifty acres and surrounded by a large field. Based on the number of dwellings, Summerlin estimated that twenty to thirty Indians lived there. The village was completely deserted, but the posse found a shirtsleeve that they thought belonged to the young boy. The search was continued for five more days, but the child was not found.[8]

Later it was learned that the child had been killed. Seminoles living in the area at first denied any knowledge of the murder, but indicated that they would assist in finding those who were responsible. "Three Indians finally proved to have committed the crime, and these the tribe willingly brought in and surrendered to Captain Casey at Fort Myers, who turned them over to civil authorities. Three days later the prisoners were found dead in jail having hung themselves."[9]

Captain Britton attempted to blame the cause of the kidnapping and murder on Summerlin. According to Britton, "Summerlane (or something like that) liv-

---

[6]David Levy Yulee, letter to Hon. James Porter. (Part of Governor Richard Keith Call's Correspondence, 13 July 1843); John Sprague, Captain, U.S. Army, correspondence with Governor William Moseley, 15 Oct. 1845, Box 2, RG101, Series 679.

[7]"Another Indian Outrage," *The News*, 2 July 1849; 28 July 1849; *The Florida Herald and Southern Democrat*, 2 Feb. 1847. Jacob Summerlin, correspondence with Governor Thomas Brown, 11 Dec. 1851; Letters from settlers at Ichepucksassa to Governor Thomas Brown regarding Seminoles, 20 Dec. 1851, Tallahassee: Florida State Archives, Box 2, RG 101, Series 755.

[8]*Ibid.*

[9]Canter Brown, Junior, *Florida's Peace River Frontier*. (Orlando: University of Central Florida Press, 1991), pp. 93-94.

ing at Hitchepuksassie [*sic*] had been out about Fort Davenport and gathering three ponies. These three ponies correspond to those of Chi-Emathla, Chop-kas party." The Indians also claimed that the horses had been stolen and that the child had been kidnapped in reprisal.[10]

It is possible that these ponies somehow became mixed in with Jake's livestock since there were herds of wild horses in Florida as late as the 1930s. Because Seminoles did not always brand their stock, it would have been easy for Summerlin to mistake Indian ponies for wild stock if the horses were not branded.[11] But, it appears unlikely that Summerlin would have stolen ponies from the Indians or anyone else—except possibly from Yankee troops during the Civil War—because such an act would have been out of character for him. This accusation surfaced at a time when the Army was generally unsympathetic to Florida settlers who complained about the Indians and could have been fabricating tales.

Summerlin was so distressed over the kidnapping that he wrote to Governor Thomas Brown complaining about the activities of the Indians in his area, "They are on our ground there is no doubt, and you may suppose our feelings when we send a child on an errand or to school. We are getting tired of waiting to see what the government will do, and we calculate to scout until we are satisfied what has become of the child, and I fear if we find the child in there [*sic*] possession there will be a fight if they don't give him up."[12]

He continued corresponding with Governor Brown about Indian hostilities and later wrote of the ambush of a mail rider that he blamed on the Indians. In the same correspondence, Summerlin asked the governor for instructions about the proper course of action to take whenever his cowboys encountered Indians outside their territory. "I would like to know, " he wrote, "what would be best for us to do for some times [*sic*] we cowhunters might come across some of them and if we have your advice, perhaps, will try and take it tough we have not gave [*sic*] the Indians any offence there [*sic*] conduct shows that they don't intend to live in peace."[13]

A year later, Summerlin co-signed a letter to Brown that was sent after "a large and respectable meeting...at Itchepuckesassa" complained about Indians roving out of boundaries and committing depredations, such as killing stock.

---

[10]Captain Britton, U.S. Army to Marshall at Fort Clinch, 3 April 1850. Tallahassee: Florida State Archives, R.G. 393, Pt. 1, West Div. and Dept., Box 4 (1850 [AW Unentered]NA); General correspondence, Florida State Archives, R.G. 593 – Series 914, Box 9 (1859-1860).

[11]In an interview with Micco (Chief) Bobby Johns Bearheart, he indicated that he was sure that Native Americans in Florida were branding their livestock in some areas—a tradition they had acquired from the early Criollo ranchers of Florida. Micco Bobby Johns Bearheart (Creek Indian Chief), Interview by author, Tallahassee, Florida, April 3, 2004.

[12]Summerlin correspondence with Governor Thomas Brown, *Ibid.*

[13]*Ibid.*

The communiqué also included the names of Captain John Parker, William Pershing, Stephen Hollinsworth, Willoughby Whitton, Captain Sparkman, B. Sparkman and Jesse Knight, the brother of Frances Summerlin.

Settlers, who sought help from the state government and the Army to remove them, exaggerated the number of Indians living in Florida during these years. Andrew P. Canova, who served with the militia during the Third Seminole War, claimed that Summerlin devised a plan to round up all the Indians in Central and South Florida by sending agents to the Indian camps to invite them to a grand festival at Fort Myers. All the tribes were invited to attend, but the plan was a failure. "Holiwangus, no good, was the sententious reply, and no amount of argument or explanation could convince them that the invitation did not arise from sinister motives."[14] It is doubtful that Summerlin ever suggested such a preposterous plan, but such had become the legend of Jake Summerlin by the late 1850s.

During this brief time of limited hostilities between the white settlers and the Indians, Jake again became a part of a scout unit — this time in Orange County, where he paid taxes on 1,200 head of cattle. The scout troop was made up of twelve men and led by Aaron Jernigan, a cattleman and one of Orange County's earliest settlers. Other members of the party included Isaac Jernigan, Needham Yates, George Hughey, C. Osteen, Captain Simeon Sparkman, T. Kinchreek [?] and two men whose last names were Bird and Lockwood. Most of these men later became prominent cattlemen or businessmen in the Orange County area. The Jernigans had complained of seeing large bodies of Indians that they suspected were stealing their cattle and starting woods fires since 1851. Summerlin, living at Hitchepucksassa, was summoned by Aaron Jernigan to help form a scout unit. The brother-in-law of Billy Bowlegs claimed that the Mikasukis, a tribe in the heart of the Everglades, drove off many of the cows.[15]

Although it was rumored that there were many Mikasukis in the area, the scouting party only captured four. The Indian prisoners were taken back to Fort Gatlin, near present day Orlando. Tragically, one of the captives, a female, hanged herself with a rope of dried bear hide. Major General B. Hopkins, who was stationed at nearby Fort Monroe, was ordered by Governor Brown to look into the circumstances of the suicide. The scouts were questioned, but Hopkins was assured that the Indians had all been and would be treated humanely as long as they did not attempt to escape. One warrior confessed that other Indians had driven cattle to the "nation," a reference to the reservation area. However, in his report to Governor Brown, Hopkins wrote, "From all the

---

[14]Andrew P. Canova, assisted by L.S. Perkins, *Adventure in South Florida*. (Tampa: Tribune Printing Company, 1906), pp. 103-104.

[15]Captain Aaron Jernigan correspondence with Governor William Moseley, 1845-1849, Box 2, RG 101, Series 679, Tallahassee: Florida State Archives, Tallahassee.

information I can procure...the Indians are disposed to remain quiet if the whites will let them alone."[16] This appraisal was hardly consistent with those of the scouts and other settlers, who argued that conditions between the factions had not improved much since the end of the Second Seminole War. The only difference, they asserted, was that there were few Indians still living in Florida. A third Seminole War would start in 1855. Summerlin would also participate in this last conflict.

Warfare had dominated much of Summerlin's life, yet by nature he was not a soldier. He considered his military service to be a duty demanded of all citizens. There were times, however, when he became a combatant to protect his own property. Having volunteered in various militia units during the Second Seminole War, he felt called upon to serve again during the Third Seminole War. In this war, he served as a scout for Captain Simeon Sparkman's volunteer company, because no one knew the territory better than Summerlin. He also acted as mediator between the federal government and the Mikasukis when the government attempted to persuade them to move to Arkansas.[17]

One of the most revealing stories about Jake's character and the devotion some people had for him happened during the war. It concerned Toby, a slave Summerlin owned, who was more of a friend than a slave or servant and was handicapped by two crooked legs. Despite this handicap, Toby was as strong as an ox and allegedly could split out as many rails as the strongest man on the frontier. Summerlin built a home for Toby and, on one occasion, Toby took in a wounded Indian and allowed him to stay in his cabin until he recovered. During his recovery, Summerlin himself frequently visited the cabin and ministered to the Indian's wounds. When he had recovered, Toby sent him on his way with potatoes and meat and asked him to keep other Indians away from Summerlin's house and from stealing his cattle. The Summerlins were not bothered that year, but as Indian hostilities increased around the Itchpocksassa area, Jake moved his family to Fort Meade. Despite the danger, Toby asked to stay behind and protect the Summerlin homestead and some of his cattle. Because Indians were normally friendly to blacks, Jake thanked him and granted him his wish. Jake returned from Fort Meade to check on Toby and found him in an exhausted state. Toby explained that two Seminoles had attempted to ransack Summerlin's home and that he had done combat with them, breaking the arm of one. As the Indians fled into the night, Toby had scolded them for "Cuming [sic] 'round a gentleman's place that way." Indians later returned and set fire to

---

[16]Major General B. Hopkins, correspondence with Florida Governor Thomas Brown, March 9, 1852, *Ibid.*

[17]William Charles Brown Diary, transcribed by Theodore Lesley, covering a period from Dec. 24, 1855 to April 9, 1856. Transcription once owned by Lesley may be in P.K. Library at University of Florida, Gainesville.

Toby's cabin and the Summerlin house, but Toby escaped. Jake later built Toby a new house near his home at Fort Meade.[18]

Perhaps the slave with whom Summerlin was the closest was Prince Johnson. About the same age as Jake, he purchased Johnson in 1863 from a Mr. Turner of Hillsborough County. The relationship between the two men was probably not unlike that which had existed between George Washington and his manservant, William Lee, who had hunted and fought together during the colonial era. Johnson was a trusted teamster before and during the Civil War and hauled goods from Tampa to Bartow for W.T. Carpenter and others. After emancipation in 1865, Johnson chose to stay on with Jake for two more years before striking out on his own. In 1871 he applied for a homestead under the Homestead Act of 1862, built his own home, along with a barn and other outside buildings, and dug his own well. Soon he was cultivating twenty acres and had a sizeable orange grove. He supported his rather large family by gradually expanding his farming operations and by digging and cleaning wells for others. When Johnson died in 1896, one obituary described him as "one of the most widely known colored men in South Florida."[19]

---

[18]John O. Parish, "The Faithful Slave," *Battling the Seminoles*. (Lakeland: Southern Printing, 1930).

[19]"Prince Johnson Dead," Obituary, Bartow *Courier*, 9 Sept. 1896.

Jake Summerlin joined the Peas Creek Baptist Church near Bartow in May 1864. He was baptized along with a female slave, whose name was Factor, by the Reverend J.M. Hayman. This church is still in existence and is the oldest Baptist Church in Polk County-founded in 1854. Jacob's wife Frances, his stepson Aaron Zipperer, a son named Jasper, a daughter and a son-in-law also became members of this church.

Chapter 5

Summerlin Expands Cattle Operations

The only means by which a young man in these tribes can rise to importance and respectability is to obtain cattle.
Rev. S.A.W. Jewett, *Livingston in Africa*, 1868

By 1854, Summerlin was paying taxes on over 2,000 head of cattle that ranged over Orange and Hillsborough Counties and 240 acres of newly purchased land. In 1852, he had also bought eighty acres of land under the terms of the 1820 Provision Act.[1]

By the late 1850s, the Florida cattle industry was beginning to grow rapidly and have a significant impact on Florida's economy. Besides the Summerlins and Knights, other sizeable herds in Hillsborough, Orange, Monroe and Manatee Counties were owned by such cowmen as William Hancock, John Lanier, Louis Lanier, John Parker, W.D. Branch, L.B. Branch, A.D. Johnston, Abner Johnston, Aaron Jernigan, Francis Johnston, W.B. Dell, John D. Young, William Wyatt, James Alderman, Fernandez Sanchez, Daniel Stone, T.R. Wells, William Whitaker and Moses Barber. Captain William Hooker of Hillsborough County had over 3,000 head of cattle. Practically all of the cattle that ranged unfettered over thousands of acres were cracker cattle or descended from Spanish stock.[2] Certainly in the 1850s, the low maintenance woods cattle were one of the most valuable commodities in Central and South Florida. While the state's cattle herds grew, cattle owners constantly sought new markets for their beeves. During the early part of the decade, Savannah was a favorite market for Florida cattle, and some cattle were sold as far away as Charleston. Of course, local sales were made in Tampa, Jacksonville, Key West, Tallahassee, St. Augustine and other scattered hamlets in the peninsula. Florida, however, was still sparsely populated and supply always exceeded demand.

Summerlin continued to be drawn to the cattle business. He loved all phases

---

[1]Hillsborough County Deed Book, 1854, Tampa, A., p. 155.

[2]Eighth U.S. Census, 1860; Schedules 1, 2 and 4; John Solomon Otto, "Florida's Cattle-Ranching Frontier: Hillsborough County," 1860, *The Florida Historical Quarterly*, July, 1984.

of it, including the cow hunts, the long trail drives, the buying and the selling. Like many pioneers, he recognized the economic potential of running cattle on vast areas of public land. In 1857, he sold his store at Hitchepucksassa, including the gins, his dwelling, forty acres of land and "a variety of domestics, saddles, and other goods suitable for country use."[3] In 1857, R.G. Dun of Dun and Bradstreet, described Jacob Summerlin as a "reliable man," with part of his taxable assets at $24,366.[4]

As the Third Seminole War wound down in 1858, vast prairies between the Kissimmee and Peace Rivers were opened for grazing. Small frontier settlements were established in this area and soon large herds roamed freely. Finding cattle markets and easy routes for driving herds to market presented major challenges to Florida cattlemen. Cattlemen lobbied to have rail lines extended to Orlando, Tampa and other terminals and, in March 1858, a group of bankers met in Ocala to discuss ways to raise money for the expansion of rail lines.[5] But nothing resulted from these meetings because of the lack of accessible liquid capital. As the decade of the 'fifties neared a close, more and more enterprising cattlemen, especially Summerlin, turned to the West Indies, notably Cuba, for new cattle markets.

As early as 1856, Captain James McKay of southwest Florida, a Scotsman by birth and an entrepreneurial powerhouse by accomplishment, started shipping cracker cattle to Nassau on his ship the *Eliza Catherine*. His first cattle shipment was loaded at Hooker's pens on the Lower Manatee River.[6] At first, cattle were loaded from the pens to the boats with large booms and leather straps — much like the early Spanish loaded cattle on their gawky caravels. Later, chutes were used, which made loading much faster but which were more dangerous to cattle. Early shipments were small, but they grew until the Union blockade almost shut exports down after 1861. In 1858, Summerlin loaded forty head for Cuba on the *Eliza Catherine*. He also shipped cattle on the *Rhoda*, the *Matchless*, the *Salvor* and the *America* between 1860 and early 1861. These ships were all des-

---

[3]*Florida Peninsular*, 30 May 1857, p. 3.

[4]Dun's firm published the famous *Dun and Bradstreet Reference Book*, a financial appraisal of companies, corporations and individuals that circulated throughout the country. The company was organized by Lewis Tappan in 1841. Any person or company listed in this publication was considered successful in the business world. Of course, at this time $24,366 in taxable assets was very high, especially in Florida.

[5]Brown, *Hart*, p. 100; Brown, *Florida's Peace River Frontier*. p. 123-126.

[6]According to Myrtle Hilliard Crow in *Old Tales and Trails of Florida*, the first shipment of Florida cattle to Cuba actually originated at Ballast Point in Tampa Bay and was hauled by McKay's ship the *Scottish Chief*. Still, according to the Theodore Lesley Papers, McKay leased a ship from the Morgan Line, the *Magnolia*, in 1858 on a bi-monthly basis at $1,500 a run to Cuba, and made the first run from Tampa. See Joe A. Akerman, *Florida Cowman, a History of the Florida Cattle Industry*, FCA (Kissimmee: 1999), 100-104.

tined for the West Indies. On the eve of the Civil War—and even during the war—Summerlin shipped only a thousand or so cows this way, but after the war, he shipped thousands of beeves to the West Indies via McKay's ships. He was not the only cattleman to send cattle to the West Indies before the war. Between May 20 and June 13, 1860, the following cattlemen shipped cattle by sea: W. B. Hooker, John Parker, B. Henry, James Green, W. Stallings, D. Sloane, William Camel, T. Summeral, W. Whiddon, the Waldons, E. Moselle, the Blockers, J. Platt, Isaac Carlton, John Pierce, James Whidden, Tom Summerall, L. Addison, the Cunliffes, S. Vanderipe, the Whitakers, the Gates, F. A. Hendry, the McNeils, the Youngs, R. Robards, James Alderman, J.A. Redd and a few others.[7] A number of these names remained identified with the cattle business, Florida politics and community growth for a long time. During the Civil War, the McKay-Summerlin association remained lucrative, and exploded once the war ended and the Cuban Revolution started in 1868.[8]

Summerlin displayed a knack for forging lasting business alliances because of his honesty, reliability and native intelligence. He was particularly conscientious about meeting deadlines and delivered livestock on time unless prevented from doing so by violent weather conditions, floods or other unmanageable circumstances. In addition to McKay, he formed business associations with such important cattlemen and businessmen as William Hooker, John T. Lesley, William B. Henderson and Eric Sloan.

In time, the resourceful and shrewd McKay recognized that he needed more ships for what he envisioned would become a highly profitable trade with Cuba. Although Texans were also sending cattle to Cuba in the 1850s, he knew the Spanish and Cubans preferred Florida beeves because of their size and flesh texture. They apparently liked the venison-taste of Florida range cattle, and they proved ideal for their spicy dishes. This difference in beef texture and taste was believed by some to be the result of Florida's grasses. In 1858, McKay began expanding his fleet by leasing a large steamer named the *Magnolia*. A year later, he purchased a ship named the *Huntress*. On the *Huntress*, he had cattle pens built on the deck. Between 1858 and 1861, McKay's ships hauled over 6,000 head of Florida beeves to Cuba.[9]

The Peninsula, a Florida newspaper, pointed out the significance of this new trade in an article that appeared in on July 28, 1860:

It may be generally known abroad that for the past year or more, Captain

---

[7]Akerman, *Florida Cowman*, pp. 101, 107, 110.

[8]Canter Brown, Junior, "Tampa's James McKay and the Frustration of Confederate Cattle Supply Operations in South Florida," *The Florida Historical Quarterly*, LXX, April 1992, pp. 411-413.

[9]*Ibid.*; Akerman, *Florida Cowman*, p. 87.

James McKay has been engaged in shipping cattle...to the Havana, Cuba market, thus creating a demand for beef heretofore unknown.
The effect of the opening of this trade is witnessed daily. Thousands upon thousands of dollars are thrown into our midst, and as necessary consequences, other branches of traffic and industry are proportionately enhanced.[10]

Summerlin and McKay worked closely together, and in December 1859, Summerlin received $3,760 from McKay for the purchases of 750 cows at roughly $5.00 per head. At this time cattle buyers were usually able to purchase cattle on the hoof for $4.00 to $8.00 a head, depending on age and quality. McKay and other shippers generally received $15.00 to $20.00 per head on delivery to Havana. Although this markup sounded high, the logistics of shipping cattle to Cuba were always complicated. All cattle destined for the West Indies were first assessed an exportation charge at Key West and, in Cuba, the Spanish often imposed heavy, fluctuating duties on imported cattle regardless of how badly they were needed. Sometimes the Spanish duty alone was $8.00 per head. While the prices of cattle were generally consistent from the ranch or farm, or point of origin, sometimes buyers paid outlandish prices. On one occasion, the Jernigans, friends of Jake Summerlin, were paid $15.00 a head by a Mr. Harvey who was collecting a herd to drive to Savannah, Georgia. Once, one of Harvey's drovers sat down in a cow pen and shelled out $3,000 in Spanish gold for 200 head of eight-year-old cows.[11]

Once McKay and Summerlin had established the market for Florida cattle in Cuba, Tampa appeared to be the most practical site for collecting and loading cattle for export. In order to hold the cattle prior to shipping, a fence was constructed "beginning on Hillsborough bay near the site of the Spanish sanitarium... extending across the peninsula about two miles north of Port Tampa, to old Tampa Bay." Existing docks at Ballast Point were modified for loading the cattle. People in the small town of Tampa were pleased with the prospect of a Florida-Cuban cattle connection, but, unfortunately for Tampa, a summer drought in 1860 resulted in the death of 2,000 pastured cattle. "Every pond and alligator hole went dry," reported James McKay, Junior. Consequently, Summerlin and McKay were forced to relocate their shipping operation to the mouth of the Peace River near present day Punta Gorda. There they con-

---

[10]"West Indian Cattle Trade," *The Florida Peninsular*, 28 July 1860.

[11]Theodore Lesley Papers; Brown, *Hart*, p. 100; Akerman, *Florida Cowman*, pp. 105, 122, 146, 168.

structed an 800-foot dock and by November 1860, started shipping cattle to Cuba.[12]

While the risks associated with loading and shipping cattle from Florida to the West Indies were high in the mid-nineteenth century, a much greater danger to this enterprise lay just over the horizon as the young state was drawn into the Civil War. Of the eleven states that eventually seceded, Florida had the smallest population and practically no manufacturing. Yet, more Floridians volunteered for the Confederate Army than were registered to vote, while a sizeable number of Floridians also joined the Union army. Everyone in the state was touched in some way by this war.

Although Florida did not have much in the way of manpower to offer the Confederacy, the state's livestock, particularly the large herds of cattle, provided its hungry and ill-clad troops with meat, leather and tallow. After the fall of Vicksburg in 1863, cattle drives from west of the Mississippi River became fewer and fewer in number and eventually stopped completely. Texas had been a major pool of cattle for the Confederacy, but by July 1863, Florida was the only source of cattle for Bragg's Army of the Tennessee and General Beauregard's southern flank.[13]

---

[12]Brown, *Hart*, p. 414; "Reminiscences of Capt. James McKay, Junior," *Sunland Tribune*, 17 (1991), 78-87; Akerman, *Florida Cowman*, 55.

[13]Tebeau, *A History of Florida*, p. 232; Akerman, *Florida Cowman*, 90.

Jacob Summerlin

This is the Jacob Summerlin, Jr. family at family reunion at Orlando in 1883. In the center are Jacob and Frances Knight Zipperer Summerlin. From left to right, clockwise, are Gideon Zipperer (stepson of Jacob), Robert Summerlin, Mary Ann Summerlin, Alice Summerlin and George Summerlin. They were identified by grandson of "Uncle Jake," Jacob Summerlin III and by his former wife, Mrs. J.G. Lawton of Bartow. (Louise Frisbee)

Chapter 6

Jake as Confederate Commissary and Confederate Soldier

Our republics cannot exist long in prosperity. We require adversity and appear to possess most of the republican spirit when most depressed.
Doctor Benjamin Rush, July 13, 1780

Florida was the third state to secede from the Union, three months before the first cannon was fired at Fort Sumter. On April 12, 1861, the irrepressible conflict of ideas and words turned into violence. Once secession became a reality, it seemed apparent that there would be a new nation.[1] Like many cattlemen living in Central and South Florida, the great issues that had separated the nation and led to the Civil War did not motivate Summerlin. He did own slaves on several occasions, but he was never interested in protecting this "peculiar institution." The few slaves that he owned were treated more like family than servants. Two at least were cowmen. One slave named Tom grew up with Jake's stepson, Gideon, and they hunted and worked cattle together. On one occasion, they scouted together to protect a wagon train from hostile Indians.[2] Like a number of Floridians, Jake supported the Confederacy because Florida had become a part of it. His friends, family and business interests were in Florida.

Jake's father had been an active Whig, had served in the territorial and state legislatures, and, though he was opposed to statehood earlier like most Whigs, became a strong unionist after statehood. Jake felt the same way, and he later wrote on his application for a presidential pardon in 1866 that he had always been opposed to secession.[3] So, too, were such Confederate icons as Robert E. Lee, "Stonewall" Jackson and James Longstreet, who also saw their first allegiance to their states. However, there were a number of cattlemen, particularly

---

[1]In his diary, Amos T. Akerman, a former resident of New Hampshire, a Southern Whig and later an officer in the Confederate Army, wrote that he joined the Confederate Army because he was convinced, along with others, that there would be a new nation, even though he was opposed to slavery and secession.

[2]John O. Parrish, "The Faithful Slave," *Battling the Seminoles.* (Lakeland, FL: Southern Printing Company, 1930), pp. 195-198.

[3]Leland Hawes, "Former Rebels Saw Error of Their Ways," Tampa *Tribune*, 3 June 1990.

in South Florida, who could never be reconciled to secession during the war. The results sometimes fostered more civil conflict and even armed dissension in the Peninsula State, creating a war within a war.

In June 1861, the Union imposed a naval blockade of Florida when the USS *Montgomery* seized Apalachicola Bay and soon a fleet had been thrown up around most of the state, which offically ended the West Indian cattle connection for the duration of the war. Still, Summerlin, now living at Fort Ogden, provided McKay with enough cattle to make illicit blockade runs worthwhile.

In order to facilitate blockade running, Summerlin constructed a crude road from Fort Ogden to Punta Gorda on the Gulf Coast. According to Mary Ida Bass Barber Shearhart in *Florida's Frontier, The Way Hit Wuz*, Summerlin and Moses Barber, with the help of James McKay and "some other smaller cow men got together and...built a corduroy road from Ft. Ogden to Punta Rassa."[4] On the small point, jutting out into the Gulf of Mexico, they built shipping pens and a dock out into the natural deep little port. When drovers neared Punta Rassa, they reached a road of cross ties of heart pine, ten feet long and ten feet wide. It was laid over a dangerous saltwater bog from where the cattle were driven into the shipping pens.[5]

Driving his cattle into pens at Punta Gorda and Punta Rassa, Summerlin and his associates would load McKay's small boat, the *Scotland Clipper*, with cracker cattle. Once loaded, McKay, long familiar with the inlets, coves and islands, would douse all his lights and quietly slip through the shallow bay into the Gulf and on to Cuba.[6] He would return with military ordinance for the Confederate Army and such commodities as flour and sugar. While the military ordinance went to the Confederate army, commodities brought a neat profit on the civilian market. It was a risky business, but neither McKay nor Summerlin ever dodged danger—particularly when it involved a cause and a potential profit. They

---

[4] Summerlin, McKay, Hendry and other cattlemen helped make Punta Rassa a rousing, flourishing port, particularly during the Cuban Revolutions. At one time, this tiny spot had been a pirate's rendezvous where the notorious [and some say, mythical] Jose Gaspar, Black Caesar and Augustus hid out in nearby coves. From there they pounced upon shipping plowing the lanes from Key West to Florida's Panhandle and westward along the Gulf Coast. The Spanish named it Punta Rassa during the 1500's, making it one of the oldest European landmarks in North America. In 1837, at the height of the Second Seminole War, a company of U.S. Marines built Fort Dulaney at Punta Rassa and named it after the Corp's first commander, Captain William Dulaney. Later that year, the Marines abandoned the fort when the Seminoles agreed to retire to a reservation south of Punta Rassa. In 1841, the installation was reactivated by the Army as the Second Seminole War heated up, but soon afterward it was destroyed by a giant hurricane that raced up the Gulf Coast. Another fort was built by army engineers nearby, which later would be named Fort Myers. In 1864, Punta Rassa was abandoned entirely by the Army. Shearthart, *The Way Hit Wuz*, pp. 193-194.

[5]*Ibid.;* Crow, *Trails and Tales*, pp. 48, 94.

[6]Crow, *Osceola Sun*, 10 June 1970.

were not about to let a Union blockade stand in their way. All commerce, however, was drastically reduced during the war and both men suffered financially.[7]

By 1861, Summerlin was one of the largest cattle owners in the state with commercial connections from the Caloosahatchee to the Suwannee. That year he purchased 10,300 head of cattle, financed by McKay, from William Hooker. Along with his cattle in Manatee, Volusia and Orange Counties and Hillsborough County, Summerlin owned over 20,000 head. By 1862 his herds produced from five to eight thousand new calves annually.[8] Despite the demand for cattle by both Confederate and Union troops and from civilians, particularly in Florida and south Georgia, his cattle holdings at the end of the war were almost as large as they had been in 1861. Because of his vast holdings and his many contacts, he was offered a commission in the Commissary Department of the Confederate government in 1861 and a contract to supply beeves. He was classified as a commissary sergeant.[9] His obligation to the Confederacy was for two years and called for 600 head of cattle to be delivered to the holding pens at Baldwin and at other railheads each week. By drawing on his own herds and by contracting with other cattlemen and farmers, he was able to supply the Confederacy with 25,000 head of beeves. He was supposed to receive from $8 to $10 per head delivered — over $200,000 in all. But it turned out to be a contribution to the Confederate cause for which he said, "I was not given a copper."[10] For those who think that Summerlin was not a patriotic Confederate citizen, they should consider this investment in money and time. Like Summerlin, many other Confederates lost all or part of their wealth, particularly when the Confederate debts were cancelled after the war. Summerlin's own circumstances were mitigated by the fact that he didn't care as much for spending money as "for the getting of it."[11]

Summerlin's support of the Confederacy did not end with merely supplying free beef for its troops. He also furnished a company of cowboy-soldiers he

---

[7]*Ibid.*

[8]Kyle VanLandingham, Personal interview, Denver, Colorado, 5 May 2004; VanLandingham and Akerman, "Florida's Early Cattle Kings."

[9]According to General John K. Jackson, with the Confederate Army in Florida, "From official and other data I learn that the product of army supplies will amount *annually* to 25,000 head of beeves, 1,000 hogshead of sugar, 100,000 gallons of syrup, 10,000 hogs [and] 50,000 sides of leather...Counting the bacon at one-third pound and beef and fish at one pound to the ration there are of meat rations...enough to supply 250,000 [men] for six months." Cited by J.E. Dovell, *Florida*, Volume I (New York: Lewis Historical Publishing, 1952), p. 496.

[10]Akerman, *Florida Cowman*, p. 85; "Geneva Historical Society Office," Orange County Historical Society Office; Robert Raylor, *Rebel Storehouse*. (Tuscaloosa: University of Alabama Press, 1995), p. 92; Dacy, *Four Centuries*, pp. 51-52.

[11]Louise Frisbie, Personal interview, Bartow, 5 May 1979.

raised with ammunition and arms. A *communiqué*, dated April 22, 1862, from Captain A. B. Noyes, who was in charge of the Second Commissary District, to Florida Governor John Milton, mentions that Captain Jacob Summerlin of Hillsborough County had purchased $1,000 of military ordinance from a Captain Kendrick of the Confederate Army. In 1864, Summerlin gave twelve horses to Captain F.A. Hendry's Company of the Cattle Guard.[12]

Confederate Business Records, M-346, Roll, #997, "Jacob Summerlin."

Nov. 1861 – 775 pounds beef — $46.50. Paid, Fernandina, Jan. 1862.

Dec. 1861 – 151 pounds beef — $9.06. Paid, Fernandina, Jan. 1862.

1862	June 20 – 401 head of beef — @$20	$ 8,020.
	June 30 – 568 "	11,360.
		$19,380.

Paid, Long Swamp, Fla., June 31, 1862

1862	July 7 – 245 head of beef @$20	$ 4,900.
10 – 238	"	4,760.
		$ 9,660.

Paid, Long Swamp, July 10, 1862.

1862	July 20 – 304	6,080.
25	247	4,940.
30	225	@22.	4,950.
		$15,970.

Paid, Long Swamp, July 30, 1862.

1862	Aug. 7 254	5,588.
10	220	4,840.
16	248	5,456.
23	199	4,378.
30	155	3,410.
		$23.672.

Paid, Long Swamp, Aug. 30, 1862.

1862	Sept. 8 244	$ 5,368.
16	151	3,322.
23	115	2,530.

---

[12]*Official Records War of the Rebellion*, Vol. LIII.

	$11,220.
Paid, Long Swamp, Sept. 23, 1862	

1862 Oct. 30 131	$ 2,882.
Paid, Long Swamp, Oct. 30, 1862	

1862 Feb. 7 – 85 lbs. soap	$17.00
½ bushel, salt	2.00
9 bushels, meal (450 lbs.)	11.25
	$30.25.

Rec., Tall, March 19, 1862.

J. A. Summerlin, Capt., 1st Fla. Cav., Travelling expense, Jan. 20 – Feb. 24, 1862.

Camp Trapin to Fernandina	27mi.	$ 2.70
Fernandina to Brooksville, Ga.	165	16.50
Brooksville, Ga., to Fernandina	165	16.50
Fernandina to Thomasville, Ga.	205	20.50
Thomasville, Ga. to Tallahassee, Fla.	50	5.00
Tallahassee to Fernandina	200	20.00
Fernandina to Jax & return	140	14.00
Fernandina to Groversville	200	20.00
Groversville via Thomasville to Tall.	80	8.00
Tallahassee to Camp Trapin	175	17.50

Paid, Tallahassee, March 22, 1862

Per diem expenses were also included for his younger brother, Captain John A. Summerlin, who helped Jake for a time with the task of transferring cattle to Confederate depots. Both men served in the Cattle Guard during the latter stages of the war.

When rail cars were not available at Baldwin, or later at Madison or Stockton, Georgia, the range cattle were driven to Savannah and Charleston. One of Summerlin's most challenging tasks in delivering beeves to these points was to find enough drovers. Cowmen liked to work for Summerlin and some took pride in claiming they were Summerlin's cowboys, but there were so many men now serving in the Confederate Army that drovers were hard to find. Consequently, General Joseph Finegan gave Summerlin permission to select thirty soldiers from Florida units to help roundup and drive cattle northward.[13] One of Sum-

---

[13]Taylor, *Rebel Storehouse*, p. 92.

merlin's drovers was his stepson, Gideon, who was a member of Company B of the 7th Florida mounted Infantry. Gideon later served in Captain F.A. Hendry's company, which was a part of the Cattle Guard.[14] Summerlin and his fifteen-year-old son, Jasper, also served in Hendry's company and both saw limited combat with this unit.

Besides his two sons, Jake also had two brothers who volunteered for the Confederate army. John A. Summerlin, a younger brother, was a captain in Davis' First Florida Regiment. He led companies that saw action in Florida, Kentucky and Tennessee. His regimental commander said of him, "He endured hardness as a good soldier and acquitted himself with honor." It was also said of him that he was a strict disciplinarian in the army and with his family. He worked mightily to bring up his children in the discipline and admonition of the Lord.[15] Information about Jake's older brother is not easily found, but a Joseph Summerlin, probably his brother, enlisted in 1861 at Vernon, Florida. His widow Elizabeth's pension application indicated that Joseph, a first lieutenant, was wounded at Murfreesboro, Tennessee, in December 1862 and died three weeks later. He belonged to Company H of the Fourth Florida Regiment.[16]

Jake set up his temporary headquarters for cattle collection at Fort Ogden. Herds were also assembled near Fort Meade. Following old Indian and military trails, the skittish cows were pushed along by the sharp cracks of the cowboy soldiers' cow whips. During the late spring and summer months, the heat was a great annoyance. Cattle drives started each day just before dawn broke. Always on the lookout for Union patrols or Confederate deserters, drovers usually rested the cattle during the hottest part of the day and then moved on until it was almost dark. Eight-and-one-half miles a day was generally considered to an adequate distance for grazing cattle to travel, but because of the demands for more and more beeves, cowmen hurried the herds at much faster rates.

Writing to Major Pleasants W. White, Chief Commissary Officer of Florida, in January 1863, Captain James McKay suggested that these cracker cattle should not be moved more than ten or twelve miles per day "as their condition generally requires great care." In his *communiqués* to White, McKay constantly complained of the poor condition of the woods cattle that Summerlin's and Hendry's drovers delivered to Madison, Baldwin, Stockton, Savannah and

---

[14]The "Cattle Guard" or the "Cow Calvary" was organized like Summerlin's unit to drive cattle to railheads in North Florida and to protect them from Union patrols and Confederate deserters. The real Cattle Guard was made up of several companies forming a battalion headed by Colonel Charles I. Munnerlin. They were extremely effective during the latter part of the war and were actually mustered into the Confederate Army.

[15]Jan Miller papers.

[16]Although Joseph Summerlin enlisted at Vernon, Florida, his birth date and his wife's name are the same on his military records as they appear on other family records.

Charleston. One of the reasons for poor condition was the lack of good pasturage caused by unusually high flood levels during these years.[17]

One Confederate drover reported that herders were fortunate to find a cow pen by the end of the day, and after the cows were penned, they might break out and stampede through the camp if they were spooked by lightening or the scream of a panther. It would take another day to round them up and get them moving again. "Such was the perversity of the beast," one cowman remarked.[18] Other obstacles in pushing cattle up the peninsula included heavy rain and windstorms. Floods were common during the spring and summer, but sometimes occurred during the fall. They often caused drovers to make wide detours with herds, extending the drives and making drovers and cattle more vulnerable to Union patrols. A flooded river could impede a herd for a whole day. Although it was estimated that there were fewer than two hundred Seminoles in Florida, some drovers even feared losing cattle to the Indians.[19]

Despite such dangers, the drovers enjoyed considerable success in delivering herds over long distances. In 1863, a detail of six men, under the command of James P. McMullen, took charge of a herd of 365 wild cows at Fort Meade and drove them to Savannah, Georgia, losing only three during the drive—a distance of over 400 miles.[20]

From November 20, 1863, to December 16, 1863, approximately 3,500 cattle were herded to Madison, Stockton and Charleston by drovers hired by Summerlin, Louis Lanier and F. A. Hendry. It was not the best time of the year to move cattle because of a lack of natural forage, but the Confederate armies were in desperate need of beeves. Sometimes as many as 2,000 head of Florida scrub cattle reached the Confederate lines each week.[21]

Like that of most soldiers who served on the frontier, a record of Summerlin's movements is difficult to find. Since he was obligated to supply the Confederacy with 600 beeves each week, most of his time was spent hunting, driving and buying cattle all the way from the Caloosahatchee River to the Kissimmee River Valley northward to railheads. One of the most interesting reports about his activities during this time appeared in the Savannah *Morning News* in the fall of 1861. According to the account, Captain Summerlin and his cowboys captured

---

[17]Brown, "Tampa's James McKay and the Frustration of Confederate Cattle- Supply Operations in South Florida," pp. 426-427.

[18]Akerman, *Florida Cowman*, pp. 88-89.

[19]"Report of the Committee on Indian Affairs," House Committee Reports. 1862, RG 915, ser. 887, Box 10, Folder 3, Florida State Archives: Tallahassee; *Records of Rebellion*, Series I, Vol. 28, pp. 459-462.

[20]Akerman, *Florida Cowman*, p. 88.

[21]*Ibid.*

a group of so-called "Lincolnites" engaged in cutting timber near Fort Myers for J. K. Stickney, who had a contract for wood with the United States. Summerlin's company succeeded in capturing four of the Lincolnites. As it turned out two of the prisoners were Frenchmen returning to France. Another was a resident of New Orleans, while the other was an immigrant making his way to Key West. Since there seemed to be no possibility of them reaching their destinations, they had hired out to Stickney in order "to shift for a living." Evidently they had no feelings about the war and they were set free in Tampa. The other two captives acknowledged that they were Yankees and opposed to "*The Cause* of the South and they were placed in confinement."[22]

After 1863, the Confederate government decided to quit contracting for cattle, but Summerlin continued his association with Captain James McKay. At the time, McKay was in charge of the Confederate Fifth Military District of Florida. His son, Richard, a Confederate officer, was also a part of this partnership. The Union blockade had become very effective, but McKay continued to smuggle a few Florida beeves to the West Indies, while Summerlin helped furnished the cargo. Between the summer of 1862 and October 1863, McKay was able to make six successful runs to Cuba.

Summerlin, who constantly combed the country for cattle, temporarily set up a dry-goods store at his home at Fort Ogden. Customers, who came from miles away, usually paid for goods with cattle. Sometimes, however, cotton was accepted when there was a scarcity of this commodity in Cuba. These operations generally proved to be highly profitable to the three men. Two ounces of Spanish gold, the typical currency, was worth about $30.00 in antebellum American money and much more in the increasingly inflated Confederate currency. An eight-dollar cow would go for two ounces of gold. On their first cooperative run to Cuba, Summerlin and the McKays grossed a profit of $18,000 in Spanish gold. But unfortunately for the three men and their customers, Union sympathizers spotted two of McKay's ships, the *Scottish Chief* and the *Kate Dale*, and reported them to Union troops, who consequently boarded both ships and burned them to the waterline.[23]

During this time, Summerlin demonstrated his compassion for widows and orphans whose husbands and fathers had been killed during the war. He sought to establish cattle herds, branded with "W" and "O," to be given to them. He started by donating 200 head, but his noble project enjoyed little success because he was unable to get enough support from other cattlemen.[24]

By the fall of 1863, the Union began to also look toward Florida for cattle and

---

[22]*Tampa Peninsula*, reprint from Savannah *Morning News*, 5 Oct. 1861.

[23]Brown, "Tampa's James McKay and the Frustration of Confederate Cattle-Supply Operations in South Florida," pp. 424-425; "Letters of James McKay."

[24]Jacob Summerlin, "Early Bartow Philanthropist," *Polk County Record*, 22 Aug. 1939.

other livestock, thus creating another supply problem for the weakening Confederacy. Florida was the principal source of beef for the Army of the Tennessee and for troops defending Charleston. In South Florida, the Civil War turned into a series of range wars as Confederate deserters and Union patrols contended with Confederate drovers and settlers whose sentiments were with the Confederacy. Absent were the orderly grand armies, such as the Army of Northern Virginia or the Army of the Potomac, made up of thousands of uniformed soldiers. On the palmetto prairies, in the pine-barrens, among the hammocks, and through the swamps of Florida, guerrilla bands, sometimes integrated with regular units, clashed with each other. They were much like the partisan units operating in the West. Small groups, operating from ambush, clashed for short periods of time. Homes were burned and livestock stolen, but what made this phase of the war so different were the ever changing loyalties of the participants. Young men who had volunteered in the beginning for the "great cause" hardly expected to be gone from home more than a few months. After the first cow hunt was over, they felt they were needed at home and some deserted. Some fled conscription but soon discovered they had to take sides in order to survive. There was little choice in the matter. Those who refused to take sides became refugees, having to constantly move or hide out from both sides. Loyalties were often confused or even changed. Some Union soldiers stationed at Fort Myers had once been Rebels, and people like Summerlin and McKay, who had done so much for the Confederacy, were accused at various times of siding with the Union. Thrown into this ferment were the real or imagined intentions of the small scattering of Indians who were courted by both sides. Only a few remnants of these once powerful tribes lived in the grass wetlands and hammocks on the outer edge of the frontier, but white settlers were still uneasy about their presence. Rumors had also circulated that Indian war parties had already attacked homesteads. Settlers and cattlemen living in this region had not forgotten the Third Seminole War and knew how a few Indians could create havoc.

Since the Confederate Army demanded that all available supplies be used to prosecute the war, settlers were apprehensive that the Indians might again take up arms to gain the basic necessities for living. Robert Taylor in *Rebel Storehouse* pointed out that Florida's commissary-general Major Pleasant White had personally seen "ragged Seminoles in dire need of cloth for clothing and ammunition for use in hunting small game." In a letter dated November 20, 1863, James McKay to Major Pleasants White, , McKay reminded White that the "goods ordered by the Indians," had still not been delivered. And as late as February 1864, McKay warned White that Union troops in Southwest Florida "might have conversation with Indians."[25] White's response was to recommend "a new government agent

---

[25]"Report of the Committee on Indian Affairs," House Committee Reports, 1862, RG915, ser. 887, Box 10, Folder 3, Florida State Archives, Tallahassee; Taylor, *Rebel Storehouse*, 304; Milton Papers: Milton to George Randolph, 16 Oct. 1862.

should be appointed to cement relations by negotiating a new compact with them as soon as possible."[26]

In 1861, the state legislature asked Governor Madison Starke Perry to appoint an Indian agent to confer with the Indians, explain why there was a shortage of trade items and to find out any intentions the Indians had regarding the war. On October 1861, he appointed "Summerlin of the county of Manatee the duly appointed Indian Agent to and for said Seminole Indians." When John Milton became governor the following year, he picked John (or Joab) Griffin to fill the position as Indian Agent. Griffin was an Ohioan who had moved to Florida, but had joined the Confederate Army shortly after Florida seceded. Earlier in 1852, he accompanied Chief Billy Bowlegs to Washington sign a treaty agreement with President Millard Fillmore.

Griffin's received orders to seek out the famous Sam Jones and Chief Tiger Tail and to allay any fears they might have of white traders cutting off trade with them. "He was also authorized to offer the state's protection and aid in the form of the system of trade providing needed staples." In turn Griffin asked Summerlin to go into the deeper reaches of the Everglades and find the great Mikasuki leader, Sam Jones. Jones was reputed to have a band of about seventy Indians. Summerlin's dealing with Indians was marked by the same honesty that prevailed in all his business dealings. "He thus won their respect and affection which was never lost. They trusted him implicitly everywhere and would ever turn to him for consultation and advice."[27]

Once he made contact with Jones, Summerlin explained how the war and the Union blockade made it difficult to provide trade supplies, especially arms and ammunition, for his tribe. This seemed to satisfy Sam Jones and he, in turn, convinced Summerlin that there had been no Indian attacks on white settlers along the frontier nor would there be. Jones even offered to establish a military alliance with the Confederates.[28] Although no Florida Indians ever became a part of the Confederate Army, A. McBride of South Carolina organized a Seminole Company of sixty-five men, known as Hodges' Company.

---

[26] *Ibid.*

[27] *Ibid.*

[28] Arpeika, Sam Jones, was one of the Mikasukis' greatest leaders. Though considered a medicine man rather than a war leader, he sometimes led his braves into battle. He was particularly conspicuous at the Battle of Okeechobee in 1837. During the Second Seminole War, his principal role was "to hold his people in the determination to fight. He had great influence." Dr. James W. Covington in *The Seminoles of Florida* said of him, "He held the most power as leader of the hardliners." At the time Summerlin met with him, he was close to 100 years old, but was still highly respected by his remaining small band. Summerlin seems to have been one of the few white men he trusted and he contacted Summerlin in 1862 "to set the record straight," denying any hostility on the part of his tribe. There is no question that Summerlin had great respect for Arpeika.

Summerlin's report of his meeting with Sam Jones evidently did little to alleviate the fears of settlers, particularly when federal soldiers made overtures to the Indians and small bands of Mikasuki began to visit Fort Myers. However, under the direction of Summerlin's friend and business partner, James McKay, Cow Cavalry units maintained contact with scattered groups of Indians and also helped keep trade contacts intact until the end of the war.

Generally the Indians had enough wisdom to remain neutral. Robert Taylor wrote in his essay, *Unforgotten Threat: Florida Seminoles in the Civil War*, "uncertainty as to their true intentions and their future actions served as the most effective weapon in the arsenal of the South Florida Seminoles during the Civil War."[29]

At Fort Myers, the Second United States Colored Troops, a crack black unit, was highly resented by refugees in the fort and by Confederates outside it. One factor that created the greatest discord in Southwest Florida was the fact that Florida had seceded and the considerable number of Unionists in this region had been afforded no say in the matter. Much of the conflict occurred in the area between Fort Meade, a Confederate outpost and Fort Myers, which was under federal control. Beginning in 1864, more and more Union soldiers were sent to Fort Myers where patrols collected and penned cattle. On March 13, thirty Union men, under Lieutenant James D. Green, were ordered to seize supplies from the area around Fort Meade "and to gather recruits from the Peace River area." After seizing goods, slaves and livestock from the Willoughby Tillis and Thomas Underhill homesteads, the detachment, which had grown to about fifty men, returned to Fort Myers.

Another guerilla raid was carried out in April when Green led a force of almost one hundred men to capture and occupy Fort Meade. Summerlin and other prominent Confederates were targeted for capture or death, but Confederate pickets spotted Green's columns about fifteen miles from Fort Meade. Captain James McKay, Junior, led a Confederate force against them in a short, but sharp, battle at Bowlegs Creek. The Union force was stopped and retired to Fort Myers. In May 1864, a Union force of 212 men from Fort Myers attacked Fort Meade. Although part of the Union column was discovered before the attack, they still managed to drive out the small group of defenders. Seizing all the supplies and livestock they could find, the Union soldiers torched the fort and retired to Fort Thompson on the Caloosahatchee River.[30]

It became evident to James McKay, Summerlin, F.A. Hendry, C.M. Boggess,

---

[29]Robert Taylor, "Unforgotten Threat: Florida Seminoles in the Civil War," *The Florida Historical Quarterly*, LXIX, January 1991, pp. 313-314.

[30]David Coles, "The Cattle Wars: The Civil War in South Florida, 1864-1865" in *Florida Cattle Frontier Symposium, 1845-1995*, (Kissimmee: Florida Cracker Cattle Breeder's Association, 1995); Brown, *Florida's Peace River Frontier*, pp. 166-173.

Streaty Parker and others that a greater Confederate presence was needed if the herds of cattle collected for Confederate troops were to reach their destination. Drovers moving cattle to northern railheads were constantly harassed by Union patrols and southern deserters, who often made off with small groups of cows.

During the spring of 1864, Summerlin and McKay contracted with the Confederate Commissary to provide beef jerky at a cost of seventy-five cents per pound. After talking to former Senator David Yulee, they decided that Bronson was the best place to set up an operation for processing beef jerky. The area had good pastures and was located close to a railroad. McKay went so far as to suggest that women in the area friendly to the Confederate cause "could be employed in this business."[31]

In early 1864, McKay and other cattlemen asked the Confederate Commissary Department to solicit the Confederate War Department for more soldiers, particularly in the Fifth Commissary District, to protect and drive the vast cattle herds that ranged over Florida. Eventually nine companies, designated as the Cow Cavalry or the Cattle Guard, were organized. They were an unusual lot and consisted of veterans from Dickinson's cavalry, settlers, ranchers and employees of the Confederate Commissary Department. Some were "cradle to grave" types, and at least one was only twelve years old.[32] Most were local residents, who could stay fairly close to their communities "where they could provide for their families." The men were loyal to the Confederacy and, most importantly, they usually knew the ground over which they rode. Their history was short, but significant, and the units remained intact even after Lee's surrender at Appomattox in April 1865.[33]

Eventually these cow cavalry companies were organized into a full battalion headed by Major Charles Munnerlyn with Captain William Footman as the executive officer. Jake Summerlin, his stepson, Gideon, and his son, Jasper, who was only fifteen years old, were members of Francis A. Hendry's Independent Cavalry Company stationed at Fort Meade. Munnerlyn rated this company as "the most efficient and reliable [one] in the battalion," and in a report to Confederate Brigadier General Miller, he claimed that this unit had been so effective that Federal troops had virtually stopped trying to confiscate cattle in the area.

While the main purpose of the cow cavalry was to protect and to deliver Florida's cattle to the Confederate Army, the units also provided a modicum of protection to settlers loyal to the Confederacy. Toward the end of the war, they

---

[31]McKay Letters.

[32]"Deaths and Funerals," Obituary for Frank Goss, *Florida Times Union*, 21 May 1934; Margaret Sawyer, relative and member of UDC, Personal interview, Tallahassee: 11 Aug. 1994.

[33]Kyle VanLandingham, historian and author, personal interview and correspondence, Denver, 6 June 2003; David Coles, "The Cattle Wars," p. 72.

engaged in purely offensive military operations directed against the federal forces at Fort Myers. Despite the fact that the Cow Cavalry had been effective, the fort and its operations were still thorns in the side of Confederate Florida. The five companies of regular troops and rangers stationed there had plenty of artillery and ammunition, which made the fort a difficult position to take. As the war was winding down, more and more refugees and deserters came to Fort Myers in search of safety and protection from active Confederate patrols. Even a party of Mikasukis reportedly parleyed there with the Union troops.

During the second week of February 1865, Major William Footman led a unit of cow Cavalry from Tampa to Fort Meade. His troops encamped near Summerlin's home, where Footman was able to organize a "battalion" of between 150 to 275 men. With Summerlin as a scout, the unit moved southward to Fort Thompson, a relic from the Indian wars located on the Caloosahatchee River. In order to reach Fort Myers, it was necessary to cross the river, which was flooded and in doing so, the troops lost most of the ammunition they carried for their one artillery piece. They marched westward toward Fort Myers hoping to launch an attack at night, but the approach to the fortress was flooded. Footman's men were able to capture the Union picket posts, but when they fired at an African American soldier who refused to surrender, the garrison was alerted and quickly unlimbered its artillery. Footman pressed for surrender, but Captain John F. Barholff, the fort's commander, refused and a firefight broke out. Realizing that continuing the assault would be futile, Footman withdrew his men in an orderly fashion and returned to Fort Meade.[34]

Florida historians have rendered several exaggerated accounts of this encounter, however, what happened at Fort Myers between the cow Cavalry and the Union soldiers stationed there was hardly more than a small skirmish. There were fewer than ten casualties for both sides and although several hundred troops were involved, no large-scale military clash ever developed. The so called "artillery duel" was between one Confederate cannon, with only a small supply of ammunition, and a Union battery inside the fort. One Confederate officer later criticized Major Footman for not establishing a full siege of the fort, but such a tactic would have been difficult to implement with only the one cannon for support and a prairie under several feet of water to cross.

Although the major theaters of the war closed in April 1865, parts of the Cow Cavalry remained on duty and in the field until June.[35] Summerlin and his two sons stayed with Hendry's company until May 5, 1865, when the unit mustered out. Summerlin was ineligible to claim U.S. citizenship at the end of the war because of his importance as a Confederate factor, especially since he had sup-

---

[34]Kyle VanLandingham correspondence regarding encounter at Fort Myers in 1865, 2 Jan. 2004.

[35]*Ibid.*

plied so many cattle to the Confederate Army. President Andrew Johnson issued a general amnesty on May 26, 1865, which "automatically restored citizenship to most rank-and-file ex-Confederates." However, Summerlin was excluded because the amnesty contained a caveat requiring a formal executive petition for ex-Confederates who were worth more than $20,000. In his petition Summerlin stated that he had always been opposed to secession and had never killed a citizen of the United States.[36]

Some Summerlin critics assert that he was not a Confederate loyalist, but a shrewd businessman who withheld cattle from the Confederate army because he was being paid in worthless Confederate scrip. This accusation, plus his petition to President Andrew Johnson, called into question his loyalty to the Confederacy. But any honest consideration of his character makes it highly doubtful that he would allow his fellow Confederate soldiers to go without food, tallow and leather merely to protect his own wealth. After all, he did provide 25,000 head of cattle to the Confederate Army for which he received no money. Other than those who lost their lives or were severely wounded, the question remains, "Which Floridian did more?"

It might be noted that such Confederate icons as Robert E. Lee and James Longstreet were also opposed to the principal of secession, but they felt a greater obligation to their states when secession became a reality. Interestingly, in 1863 Summerlin owned twelve slaves. Robert E. Lee owned none. It is doubtful that Summerlin, or most cattlemen in Central and South Florida, was interested in preserving the peculiar institution of slavery. In her dissertation, *Black Society in Spanish St. Augustine, 1784-1821,* Jane Landers points out, "On the frontier, race was a concept modified by social connections, wealth and behavior and upward mobility was not as difficult as it may have been in a major colonial center."[37]

When Summerlin joined the Baptist Church of Christ at Peas Creek in May 1864, he was joined by "Factor," his female slave. It seems likely that if Summerlin's Confederate loyalties had been questioned in 1864, he would not have joined or even been accepted in this particular church The minutes of the service indicate that "After the preaching of a sermon by Elder J.M. Hayman, an opportunity was given for persons to unite with the church—when Factor, a woman belonging to Jacob Summerlin presented *themselves,* and each stating experience of grace, were duly received and were baptized by Elder J.M. Hayman." Jacob's wife, Frances, his stepson, Gideon, his son, Jasper, a daughter and a son-in-law also became members of this same church. Membership of the

---

[36]Leland Hawes, Tampa *Tribune,* 3 June 1990; Microfilmed letter from Jacob Summerlin to President Andrew Johnson requesting executive clemency: P.K. Yonge Library at University of Florida, Gainesville.

[37]Brown, *Florida's Peace River Frontier,* p. 140.

Baptist Church of Christ at Peas Creek also included members of the Cow Cavalry such as F.A. Hendry, F.C.M. Boggess, John F. Fewell, J.J. Blount, William R. Flint, W.B. Varn, William Altman and Soloman Godwin.[38] The strictness and severity of this church's discipline can be seen in what happened to F.C.M. Boggess, who, despite his prominence as a Confederate officer, was kicked out of the congregation when someone claimed they saw him drunk.[39]

Perhaps the greatest recognition of Summerlin's faithfulness to the Confederacy came from the enemy. A Federal officer, Captain Henry Crane, who was stationed at Fort Myers described Summerlin as "the notorious Jake Summerlin, the great cow driver, the Indian Agent, etc., and one who has done more for the Confederacy and more injury to us, than to any other of his position." Crane also declared that Federal troops had driven him [Summerlin] from his home and threatened death and destruction to his family and, he added, "This is as I would have it, and the poison works finely."[40]

During the war, Summerlin and his family moved from Fort Meade to Fort Blount in present day Polk County, which had been a fort during the Third Seminole War. He purchased 179 acres from Riley Blount of Polk County on June 25, 1862, for $3,000 in Confederate money. The first settlement in this area came in 1851 when several families, which included such notables as Riley Blount, Streaty Parker and John Davidson, had moved into the immediate region. Blount owned the greater part of the property that would become the town site.[41]

One of the problems that faced Polk County residents in 1861 was where the county seat would be located. While most of the nation was caught up in the ebb and flow of the Civil War, citizens of Polk County were more concerned with local issues, especially finding a location for a permanent county seat. A newly elected county commission, made up of William S. Harris, James Hamilton, Isaac Waters and Joseph Mizell, met on June 18, 1861, at Mud Lake, northwest of present day Highlands City. Despite the natural beauty of the area, the Polk County electorate desired a more central location. They chose Jefferson, located about a mile south of Old Fort Blount, but they were unable to secure title to the land. As the war became more widespread and the volunteer musters became more frequent, the problem of a county seat was placed on the back burner.[42]

---

[38]VanLandingham Papers, Denver.

[39]*Ibid.*

[40]Captain Henry Crane, Copies of letters of Henry Crane of Union Army during Civil War. P.K. Yonge Library, University of Florida, Gainesville.

[41]Brown, *Florida's Peace River Frontier*, p. 92.

[42]*Ibid.*, pp. 144-145; M.F. Hetherington, *History of Polk County, Florida*, (St. Augustine: 1928. Reprint Chuluota, FL: 1971), p. 313.

Jacob Summerlin

During the war, the Confederate States Postal Service selected Fort Blount as the site for a post office and local residents were encouraged to choose a new name for the station. The Reverend Robert N. Pylant proposed "Bartow" to honor the Confederate general Frances Stebbens Bartow — killed at the Battle of First Manassas. The locals accepted the proposal and the small town that grew up around the post office would thereafter be known by this name.

When the war ended in April 1865, a new county commission returned to the knotty point of locating a county seat. The state was unable or unwilling to provide a site, and no individual seemed to have a solution. This was not an unusual situation all over the former Confederate states where so many new social, political and economic forces were in conflict.

According to Canter Brown in *Florida's Peace River Frontier*:

> Into the vacuum formed by the state's inability to act stepped Jacob Summerlin. Having purchased for its development potential in 1863 the 160-acre Riley R. Blount homestead at Bartow, Summerlin offered in October 1866 to give [his] lands at Fort Blount.[43]

The forty acres were designated for use by the county and the problem appeared resolved. Summerlin, however, went further and circulated a petition stating in part:

> All persons in favor of haveing [sic] the County Cite [sic] for Polk County located at this Elligible [sic] point will please sign this Petition to be presented to the Judge of Probate and County Commissioners for their approval.[44]

Summerlin's donation of land would significantly affect the history of Bartow and Polk County. Sixty-seven Polk County residents signed the petition, which was later approved by the county commission. Within a month, Representative Daniel Stanford introduced a bill to formalize the selection of Bartow in the Florida House of Representatives where, with the endorsement of Senator F.A. Hendry, it was approved. The deed was done. On June 15, 1867, the Polk County Commissioners contracted with John McAuley to construct a thirty-by-forty foot, two-story courthouse on the land. As Canter Brown said about Bartow, "The community owed its existence, in great part, to the patronage of a cattleman, Jacob Summerlin."[45] The United States government did not accept the name of Bartow until 1880. In time, it would become one of the most beautiful

---

[43]Brown, *Florida's Peace River Frontier*, p. 186.

[44]*Ibid.*

[45]Canter Brown, "Philip and Morris Dzialynski: Jewish Contributions to the Rebuilding of the South," *American Jewish Archives*, XLIV, Fall/Winter, 1992, p. 524.

cities in Central Florida.

Summerlin built a home for his family on the Old Lakeland Road in 1862. He also planted a small orange grove there and, after the war, hired Seminoles to cultivate and manage the trees. Unfortunately, his first home burned to the ground, but he built a new residence in the village of Bartow. Five generations of Summerlins would live in this house.[46]

While Jake was away from his Bartow residence so much of the time buying and driving cattle, Indians working on the place would move their small chickees close to the Summerlin house. At first this evidently frightened Mrs. Summerlin, but she later learned they were trying to protect her during Jake's absence. The Seminoles who worked for the Summerlins appeared to have a fondness for her gentle ways, and they referred to her as "pretty white faced squaw," in apparent appreciation for her appearance as well as her kindness.[47]

In 1867, Bartow was divided into lots, and Summerlin decided to donate 120 acres of the land he had bought in the small town to be used for churches, a school and public buildings. He gave twenty acres to the Baptist Church and another twenty acres to the Methodist Church. There is no record that Summerlin belonged to either of these churches, but he continuously supported them financially and later did the same for two churches in Orlando. Furthermore, he specified that forty acres of his gift was to be used for education purposes, and the remaining forty acres was to be used by the county government for public buildings. There seemed to be no end to Summerlin's philanthropy and in the same year, "he built a frame, two-story twenty-five by forty-foot building known thereafter as the Summerlin Institute. The first floor for years was used as a school and church, while the upper floor served as a Masonic hall. Other strong structures were built close by, some by Jake's stepson, Gideon Zipperer." The lumber for all this construction came from a steam sawmill Summerlin had earlier purchased in St. Augustine, shipped to Tampa and hauled with oxen to Bartow, where it was set up at Carpenter's Pond. Teams of oxen, two or three yokes to the wagon, were used for this Herculean task. The importance of the durable ox in the settlement of Florida cannot be overstated. They were particularly significant in the timber business and were used well into the twentieth century.[48]

When one considers the creation of the Summerlin Institute, the land he provided for churches and the role he played in establishing a county seat, Summerlin certainly deserved the title of "Bartow's City Father."

Summerlin's mill operated from six to ten years. While timber was generally abundant and free, lumber had to be purchased. As late as 1932, homes were

---

[46]Louise Frisbie, "The Bartow Years," *Polk County Democrat*, 25 Oct. 1973, Part Seven.

[47]*Ibid.*

[48]Brown, *Florida's Peace River Frontier*, p. 45.

still standing and being used that had been built with Summerlin's lumber.

When the war ended, Middle Florida, where a slave driven economy had existed, shifted mostly to small, diversified farms. The state's economy experienced a severe depression and property values decreased greatly—more in Florida than even in war torn Virginia. But freedmen, more than any other group of Floridians, suffered more from the depressed economy, since they were generally not property owners nor had any other means of support. In South and Central Florida, however, the livestock-citrus based agriculture did not change that much and large herds of cattle still roamed across the flatlands. G.F. Thompson, inspector of the Freedman's Bureau of Refugees and Abandoned Lands on tour of Central and lower West Coast Florida in December 1865, reported that Jacob Summerlin of Polk County was the largest stock raiser in the region. His cattle herds were estimated at between 15,000 and 20,000 head, valued at $75,000—a small fortune then.

Thompson recalled seeing many cowboys who were employed by Jacob Summerlin and who took pride in working for him. Describing these cowboys, he said, "The natives are brought up to this business from youth, know little else, and like nothing better than to be given a horse, a dog [cow dog] and the care of the herd." Most of the cattle they tended were shipped to Cuba, but some were destined for Savannah, Charleston and even New York.[49]

A correspondent with the Sandersville *Georgia-Herald*, reported some years later that these Florida cowboys were "generally well mounted on nimble ponies with large water proof saddlebags filled with rations for themselves and feed for their horses, and all with the indispensable double-barrel shotgun or repeating rifles, and ammunition strapped across their shoulders. They are a *sui generis* class and are recognized as soon as seen. The party often takes a wagon with supplies of corn, oats, the inevitable hominy or grits, coffee, flour and salt for the game they kill. By their nomadic life, they are fine riders and show themselves men of strong will and solid sense. They are pleasant and affable to strangers, but doubtless would prove rough customers if bad blood was raised."[50] This correspondent drew quite a different picture of the cracker cowboy than Frederick Remington did in 1895. With his pictures and his prose, Remington presented these cowboys as ignorant and indolent.[51]

According to James Covington, Summerlin employed every man within 50 miles of the port of Tampa in 1865 to round up cattle for the West Indies, Key West, Savannah and Charleston. Captain James McKay, the "kingpin of cattle shipping," who had lost his small fleet during the war, managed to acquire

---

[49]"Cattle Trade with West Indies, Key West, Savannah and Charleston," *Florida Peninsular*, 18 Aug. 1869.

[50]*Weekly Floridian*, dates missing. Bronson Papers.

[51]Frederick Remington, *Harpers New Monthly Magazine*, June 1895.

replacement boats by 1866 and took his first load of cows from Manatee to Havana that same year. Aboard were some of Summerlin's cattle. This marked the revival of a major commercial prewar enterprise and greatly added value to Florida's economy when the cattlemen were paid with Spanish gold doubloons. Florida, like the rest of the former Confederate states, was left without much hard real currency when Confederate debts had been cancelled, and the lack of a viable system of currency seriously hampered the revival of the state's economy. Spanish gold, as always, was a very acceptable form of money and the renewal of the cattle trade proved to be a financial windfall for parts of Florida.[52]

Property values had dropped over 47% from their 1860 level, but cattleman F.A. Hendry figured that there was as much as a 15% profit on capital investments in the cattle-to-Cuba connection. And there were plenty of cracker cattle to be sold. A special agent for the Freedman's Bureau made the following report in 1866 after visiting south Florida:

> After very thorough inquiries of the most intelligent stock owners, both east and west of the Kissimmee River in probable number of cattle grazing through this district, I place the estimate at 150,000 head. When an entire stock is sold, the ruling price is $6.00 per head; this would make a total value of $900,000. Cattle for the Havana market brings from $14.00 to $18.00 in gold, at the point of shipment.[53]

For the entire state, the number of cattle was estimated to be over 463,000 head with a total value of $3,089,000. By 1873, there were approximately 500,000 head of cattle in Florida valued at $4,322,000. Florida's Reconstruction government was quick to recognize the potential of Florida's livestock herds as a tax revenue source and soon began to impose sizeable assessments on them.[54]

In 1867, Summerlin decided to move temporarily to Liberty County, Georgia, so that he could provide his children with the advantages of a formal education. Not until 1868 did the state government in Florida meet the requirements of the 1867 Reconstruction Acts to provide a uniform system of common schools. On January 30, 1869, the legislature enacted a statewide comprehensive school law, but it would be years before adequate funding occurred.

There were a few schools scattered throughout the state, such as the Quincy Academy and a similar school at St. Augustine. There was even a school at Bartow "under the tutelage of a lawyer and Baptist minister named Samuel C.

---

[52]James W. Covington, *The Story of Southwest Florida*, Vol. II, (New York: Lewis Historical Publishing Co. Inc., 1957.)

[53]Akerman, *Florida Cowman*, p. 104; Theodore Lesley Notes.

[54]*Ibid.*, pp. 105-107.

Craft." And, of course, there were the Freedman's Bureau schools, but evidently Jake was more impressed with the Walthourville Union Academy at Flemington, Georgia. It had a broad curriculum and was reputedly "one of the best academies in the South." Geography, Latin, grammar, arithmetic and composition were offered. The academy had been established in 1834 and was supervised by a member of the local plantation families. Professor Charles E. Cook, a graduate of Mercer University, was the principal for a long time. Tuition was only $1.00 per month per student for primary and intermediate classes. The school was housed in a building that had been donated by the Congregationalist and Baptist churches. Four of Jake's children—George, 21 years old; Robert, 17 years old; Samuel, 15 years old, and Alice, 12 years old—attended the academy during the four years the family resided in Georgia. Jake was listed as a stock raiser in the 1870 U.S. Census for Glynn County, and his son, Jasper, who was 23, was listed as a drover. Three other people were also listed as part of the Summerlin household. They were Mary Ann or "Mollie," their oldest daughter who was married to a Mr. Fewell, and their son, Edward. Adolphus Brooks, who was probably a boarder, was also listed.[55]

Parts of Jake's large Florida cattle operations were left in the hands of Gideon Zipperer, who was now a very mature twenty-four year old. He also maintained an association with David Hughes and Julius Rockner who were buying and sending cattle to the West Indies and Key West. Periodically, Jake and Jasper made trips by horseback to Central and South Florida. On August 15, 1869, the *Florida Peninsular* of Tampa reported that there were two schooners engaged in shipping beef cattle from Fort Ogden to Havana and that "Colonel" Summerlin had a contract for shipping 1,500 head from the same point to the Cuban city. The article further suggested that with the opening of the Havana market and with the new demand for Florida beef in New York, "the stock owners in South Florida will be able to dispose of all their saleable beef this fall."[56]

Through the efforts of Captain F.A. Hendry, Summerlin's company commander during the Civil War and one of Fort Myers' favorite sons, New York started to look to Florida for part of its beef supply. Cattle destined for America's great port were generally driven to Palatka on the St. Johns River where they were loaded on steamers bound New York. During one period, 1,200 head per month left Palatka for the North. Most of these cattle were tough, lean woods cattle, or cracker cows, descended from Spanish stock. They were some-

---

[55]Louise Frisbie, "Years After Leaving Home," Part 6, 22 Oct. 1975, p. 145; Virginia F. Evans, *Liberty County, A Pictorial History*, (Statesville, GA: Liberty County Board of Commissioners, 1979); Walthourville Union Academy, Georgia Dept. of Archives and History, Atlanta; Robert L. Groover, *Sweet Land of Liberty, A History of Liberty County, Georgia*. (W.H. Wolfe Associates, 1987.)

[56]"Cattle Trade with West Indies, Key West, Savannah and Charleston," *Florida Peninsular*, 15 Aug. 1869; 22 Sept 1869.

times known as *wiregrass cattle* or *4-H cattle*—hide, hair, hoofs and horns.[57]
Jake was in Savannah looking for potential cattle buyers when the following
item appeared in the *Florida Peninsular* on September 22, 1869:

We learn that Colonel Summerlin who is now in Savannah, finds that a
much better market for cattle than Cuba, and had telegraphed his friends at
Bartow, that for the future, he will drive all his beef cattle to Savannah. We
are truly glad to know this—to know that our stock owners have found a
market instead of Havana, which at all times had been uncertain and fluctuating.

The significance of the Savannah market during this time was echoed by Mrs.
Oregon Hendry Blount, whose family ran cattle along the Alafia River at the
end of the Third Seminole War:

Life went on much as before. The river was full of fish and the forest full of
game. Deer meat was so common the family seldom ate it, but fed it to the
dogs.
The cattle multiplied. Savannah, nearly 500 miles away, was the big beef
market of that day and Oregon's stepfather and brothers were often gone for
months on a drive to that city. Later the Cuban trade developed and shipments were made from Punta Rassa, near Fort Myers.[58]

The Cuban market for Florida cattle had been active as early as 1856, but it
did fluctuate just as other cattle markets did, however this has been the pattern
of cattle markets all over the United States. But from the 1850s to the end of
World War I, the Cuban markets were usually good to the Florida cowmen.
During the Civil War, the shipment of cattle to Cuba from the Sunshine State
dropped to a trickle, but in 1867, a total 7,089 were shipped to the island. In
1868, the number of exports to Cuba fell to 3,000 because of the Spanish import
duty of seven dollars per head. But this changed again in 1870 and Summerlin,
David Hughes and Julius Rocker shifted part of their operations to Punta Rassa
and were shipping out "a cargo weekly," after the Cuban demand for beef
exploded when the effects of an insurrection began to be felt in Cuba's cattle
producing regions.

---

[57]"New York Cattle Trade," *Ibid.*, 11 Aug. 1869; D.B. McKay, "Story of Mrs. Blount Recalls
Rugged Days," *Tampa Sunday Tribune*, 26 Sept. 1948.

[58]Brown, *Florida's Peace River Frontier*, pp. 198-199; *Florida Peninsular*, 26 May 22 July, 11
August, 8 and 22 September and 23 October, 1869.

Many able bodied men of practically all ages served in militia units during the Second Seminole War (1835-1842). Although still in his teens, Jacob Summerlin, served in several Florida companies during this time. Most encounters consisted of short guerilla attacks by Florida's Native Americans as shown in this illustration. (Illustration by Joe Akerman)

photograph on right
Francis and Jake Summerlin around 1890. (Orlando Historical Society)

photograph below
Orlando, circa 1893, known as the town that Jake Summerlin helped build.
(Florida State Photographic Archives)

photograph on left

Captain F. A. Hendry, who commanded a unit of the famous "Cow Cavalry" during the Civil War, was a legendqary figure among Florida's cowmen.
(F. A. Hendry Reunion Collection)

photograph below

Aaron Gideon Zipperer, Jake Summerlin's stepson, who had large cattle herds and orange groves, circa 1880.
(Florida State Photographic Archives)

photograph above and below

Jake Summerlin, to the right of the hoist, at the dedication of the cornerstone to the Summerlin Institute, May 12, 1887. The faculty, student and other guests are pictured below. (Florida State Photographic Archives)

Jake Summerlin is surrounded by members of his family, faculty members and guests on the front steps of the Summerlin Institute in 1888.
(Florida State Photographic Archives)

This is the only known photograph of Jake Summerlin dressed in a formal coat and tie. He preferred to dress as a cracker cowman.
(Florida State Photographic Archives)

A posed photograph of Jake Summerlin, probably taken in the 1870s, has generated some speculation that this was not really Summerlin. Part of the skepticism about the picture is based on the fact that he did not smoke. Generally, however, the picture is accepted as authentic and the pipe is regarded as only a photographer's prop. (Florida State Photographic Archives)

The Summerlin "home-hotel" in Orlando, was a landmark for sixty-six years before it was razed. Built in 1875, the hotel enjoyed a favorable reputation among travelers to the "City Beautiful." (Florida State Photographic Archives)

Jake Summerlin built the Orange County Courthouse in 1875 in order to defeat a bid by General Henry S. Sanford to make Mellonville (Sanford) the county seat. (Florida State Photographic Archives) *photograph above*

F. A Hendry built this bivouac for cowmen at Punta Rassa, circa 1880. This building was adjacent to an international telegraph station that allowed cattlemen to keep in contact with their customers in Cuba. (Photograph in possession of the authors) *photograph above*

Francis (Fannie) Knight Zipperer Summerlin. (Florida State Photographic Archives) *photograph above. .*

Bartow, Florida, circa 1890. (Florida State Photographic Archives) *photograph above*

Chapter 7

One of Orlando's Early Visionaries

In 1873, Summerlin decided to move back to Florida—this time to the small hamlet of Orlando. His children had completed six years of formal education at a well-respected academy, and Orlando was near the center of his Florida cattle operation. But perhaps the main reason he chose Orlando was because of his wife's failing health. Orlando had a reputation as a haven for those who suffered from respiratory problems because it was thought to be drier and higher than other parts of the state.[1]

When Jake led his several wagons filled with family and furnishings into Orlando in 1873, the population of the tiny village was only seventy-eight persons. It had been reported five years earlier that Orlando had two log stores, a log courthouse and a few cabins. Settlers had lived in the immediate area since 1840 when Owen Simmons, formerly of North Carolina and Jacksonville, built a cabin in the Lake Holden area. Land was available for homesteading under the Armed Occupation Act and much of unoccupied Florida appeared inviting to farmers and cattlemen. Simmons was married and had served in the Second Seminole War, which was probably when he became familiar with the potential advantages of this area of the state. The following year, he persuaded a friend of his and of Summerlin's, Aaron Jernigan, to move from Georgia to the Lake Holden area. Aaron also brought his brother, Isaac.

The area where Aaron Jernigan settled was named "Jernigan" in his honor. The name of the settlement was changed to Orlando in 1857. According to legend, it was named after a soldier named Orlando Reeves, who was killed during the Second Seminole War while acting as a sentry for his company. His quick response in sighting a Seminole war party presumably saved the rest of the company. [There is no certainty regarding the location of his gravesite, but when I grew up in Orlando during the 1930s and 1940s, the general opinion was that Reeves was buried close to Lake Eola.][2]

---

[1]Crow, *Old Tales and Trails*, p. 17.
[2]*Ibid.*, pp. 14, 17.

The Jernigans brought a sizeable herd of cattle with them when they moved and, by 1852, Aaron declared ownership of 1,500 head for taxation purposes in Orange County. Although Summerlin did not live in Orange County in 1852, he affirmed ownership of 1,200 head of cattle there for tax purposes. He also had several thousand head in other counties that year.[3]

Summerlin was very familiar with the topography of the region, the military and Indian trails that provided easy travel and the advantages of raising livestock in the Orlando area. He had served as a scout throughout central Florida during the Second Seminole War. In 1847, he had led a survey party from Mellonville, today's Sanford, to map a possible canal route across the state. In 1851, Jake was already running 1,000 head of cattle in Orange County. As early as 1854, records show he had sold $6,500 worth of beef to Robert Barnhart, and in 1857, he purchased 1,500 head of cattle at Geneva—not far from modern day Orlando.[4]

Also in 1852, Jake had been a part of a scouting party operating out of Fort Gatlin in search of Seminoles who were allegedly taking cattle from the Jernigans and setting fires throughout the region. During the Civil War, Summerlin often traveled through Orange County and other parts of central Florida to purchase cattle to meet his quotas for the Confederate Army and for a few cattle to ship to the West Indies.

One of Summerlin's first contributions to the people of Orange County, and there would be many, was to help settle one of the worse range wars in Florida's history. Unlike many other conflicts during this period, race was not a factor in the dispute, which centered on the animosities that grew out of Reconstruction. The "feud" that developed was strictly political and familial in nature. The two principal families involved were the Barbers and the Mizells. Both clans were old-line Florida pioneers, and their feud was what Jim Bob Tinsley called a "hereditary quarrel" in *Florida Cow Hunter* When Jake moved to Orlando, the worst part of this dispute was over—at least the killings. David Mizell, a Confederate veteran, had been appointed Orange County sheriff by the state Republican government, and his brother, John R. Mizell, had been appointed the judge of Orange County's civil and criminal courts. The Barbers, like many white Southerners, resented the Reconstruction government and when they thought exorbitant taxes were levied on their cattle, they refused to pay. When Sheriff Mizell confiscated some Barber cattle for payment of taxes, all hell broke loose. Moses Barber, an unreconstructed Confederate, whose cattle ran from Canoe Creek Island for thousands of acres north and south, issued a warning to all Mizells to stay off his property. A grand jury indicted Barber

---

[3]Orange County, Tax Rolls, 1852.
[4]Wayne Miller, "Shifting Scenes in Florida," *The Gazette*, 27 Feb. 1936.

on a number of charges, including tax evasion, arson, adultery, forcibly confining and falsely imprisoning George Bass, a friend of the Mizell clan. Sheriff Mizell was instructed to arrest him on these charges. The Barbers, in turn, claimed the Mizells had stolen cattle from their herds. One thing led to another and Sheriff Mizell was murdered. Before the violence had ended, eight people had been killed.[5]

By the time Summerlin settled in Orlando, while the killings had ended, the animosities were still there, and the situation was still very explosive. Besides the murders involving the Barber-Mizell feud, cattle were being rustled all over Central Florida. Rustling was a major concern for the grand jury when it met in Orange County and "Violence continued over the next several years (after 1870) as the cattle industry expanded, but some amity was on the way." Summerlin and other cowmen gradually brought order to the local industry by improving the county's method of registering marks and brands, which had been rather haphazard before. Prominent cattlemen also took turns serving as inspectors. There were still occasional thefts, "but the wholesale rustling of herds became uncommon."[6]

Orlando's central location, its nearness to waterways and its junction with several military roads and cattle trails gave the settlement a tremendous potential for commercial development, but when Jake and his family moved there, there were no railroads. Jake's close friend, Ossian B. Hart, a newcomer to Florida politics and a strong proponent of expanding railroads into the interior of the state, was elected governor in 1873. Summerlin probably thought tracks would soon be crisscrossing Central Florida after Hart's election, but Hart died in 1874 before any tracks could be laid. Efforts to get rail construction underway were foiled by the so-called "Vose injunction," which made it almost impossible for the state to raise monies for internal improvements. Land had been Florida's chief revenue source, but an investor, Francis Vose, had been an original investor in the Florida Railroad in 1870. He accepted bonds in payment for railroad iron, but then he secured a court order forbidding payment for land in anything but hard currency. When state land sales continued without payments to creditors, Vose and his associates persuaded the courts to place the lands in receivership which required the consent of the bondholders before any sales could take place. Vose threatened to take over all the state lands or to force a public sale. Fortunately for Florida, Hamilton Disston, a Philadelphia millionaire, came to the rescue and purchased four million acres of land in South-central and South Florida from the state at twenty-five cents an acre. The

---

[5]Jim Bob Tinsley, "These Killings are Known as the Barber—Mizell Feud," *Florida Cow Hunter.* (Orlando: University of Central Florida Press, 1990), pp. 17-31; Jerrell H. Shofner, *Orlando the City Beautiful.* (Orlando: Douglas S. Drown, 1995), pp. 33-35.

[6] *Ibid.,* p. 41.

bondholders were paid off and the state was able to obtain a "clear" title to the encumbered property. The state's sale of sixteen million additional acres in 1880 provided needed funds for railroad construction.[7]

Jake was disappointed, as were other cattlemen and business people, that it took so long to get railroad building started, but in 1880, the South Florida Railroad began construction. Soon, dozens of other railroad companies had projects underway. Longwood, located about twelve miles from Orlando, became the junction for three railroads in the 1880s. A logging tram road at Longwood was converted into a commercial track and expanded into the Orange Belt Railroad, which ran all the way to St. Petersburg. By 1885, Orlando had become a railhead and large herds of cattle, driven up from the Peace River Valley and the Kissimmee River Valley, were loaded there on trains bound for major markets.[8]

Summerlin had not been in Orlando long before he and W.A. "Bill" Patrick bought Doyle Brantley's mercantile business. Although W.A. Lovell had opened Orlando's first mercantile establishment in 1886, which was a smallish fourteen feet by sixteen feet in size, the Summerlin-Patrick store building was actually built in 1871. It was forty feet by sixty feet, was the largest storefront located in Orlando at the time and was located about two hundred feet from the old post office building. Both Jake and Bill Patrick were gifted entrepreneurs. Summerlin and Patrick made trips to Savannah, usually buying about $25,000 worth of stock, which was shipped by water all the way to Mellonville. From there, Henry L. Meeks hauled their goods to Orlando by wagon using the old Fort Mellon-Fort Brooke Trail. The wagon haul took a yoke of six oxen. Part of their stock included barrels of whiskey, which were retailed in quarts or larger quantities. The dry goods and fancy merchandise that made up about seventy-five percent of the stock were hauled first. Then Bill Patrick returned to Mellonville for the balance of the stock. Most of the goods were displayed in the store in a group of twenty-four cases with glass fronts.[9]

In the immediate postwar period, merchandise was seldom sold for cash. Sales were recorded in books and debts were most often settled through a system of bartering. Customers bought necessities and paid for them with hogs, cattle, timber, citrus or vegetables. Banking, as we know it today, was nonexistent in Orlando. Commercial transactions often involved very creative methods of payment. Notes of various descriptions were used all over the frontier. Typical of the types of exchange used was one signed by William C. Brown, who had been a clerk in Jake's store at Cork. The note read, "I will pay the bearer ten cents in current bills when presented in sums of five dollars and upward at

---

[7]Tebeau, *A History of Florida*, p. 41.

[8]Crow, *Old Tales and Trails* pp. 13, 25; Shofner, *Orlando the City Beautiful*, pp. 38-39, 41, 48, 50, 56.

[9]Crow, *Old Tales and Trails*, p. 50.

Cork, Florida." At Alafia, a place Summerlin often visited, the following scrip issued by A. Wordhoff during the Civil War read "payable to bearer in current Bank Bills, when presented in sums to amount of five dollars." These bills were all of the same general design and had the "value [of the note] at each end in different styles and type and a center vignette, which ranged through several types of ships, a railroad train and a horse drawn wagon." This same style of scrip was also printed in 1862 for businesses in Bayport, Brooksville, Hernando County, Manatee, Orange Spring and Tampa.[10]

Of all his achievements, Summerlin was above everything else a skilled and successful businessman. His early experiences at his trading post at Itchepuck-esassa were undoubtedly helpful, and he did well in Orlando. Jake still operated his cattle business, buying cattle all over Central Florida and North Florida into St. Johns County. During the 1870s, he began to turn over much of his cattle operations to his son, Sam. Cattle continued to be driven to Punta Rassa, a location sometimes known as Summerlin's Port, where Jake owned almost 1,000 acres of holding pens and a large wharf with cattle chutes. Most of the cattle were destined for Cuba and cattlemen like the Summerlins were still being paid in Spanish gold.

Jake built a home, which was completed in 1874, in Orlando for his family. It was the largest house in the community and the Summerlins often took in roomers, a custom for the times. Their residence became so popular with the growing influx of newcomers that Jake decided to remodel it, expand it even more and turn it into a hotel. He spent over $15,000 on the project—a tremendous sum for the times—and the Summerlin Hotel was completed in 1875, the same year that Orlando was incorporated as a town. The building soon became a famous landmark in Orlando and "remained a great attraction for 66 years, and was woven into the romance that became Orlando."[11]

Jake never did anything halfway—nor did his wife Fannie—and they went to great lengths to see that their guests were comfortable. Orlando was mosquito country, and when the hotel first opened, a sign placed on the front desk promised guests ten cents for each mosquito caught in the hotel. It was said that not a cent was ever paid to any customer. Their secret for intimidating the pesky insects was never revealed. "Rates at the hotel were generally two dollars daily which included the delight of eating at a table loaded with garden vegetables." "The meats," according to Dena Snodgrass, "were pork, beef and venison that were brought there by the Indians...and there was plenty of fresh milk—Jake

---

[10]Mary Johnston, *Pioneers of the Old South*. (New Haven: Yale University Press, 1918), p. 233.

[11]*Osceola Sun*, 18 Sept. 1975; Akerman, "Jacob Summerlin," *Florida Pathfinders*, p. 121.

kept a number of cows penned in a plot nearby which later became a sweet 'tater patch.[12]

Postmen were seldom seen in the area before 1880, and when the first one arrived at the Summerlin Hotel, "he was roundly welcomed, gently and considerately escorted to a room on the third floor." But after the postman left for Fort Mellon, the room was thoroughly deloused with a bath of kerosene as postmen were known for carrying bedbugs because they had to sleep in all kinds of quarters on their rounds.

The rustic village's social life centered around the Summerlin family. Jake's daughter, Alice, the widow of James Davet of Bartow, was called "Belle" and she was very popular. She was a good pianist and owned the first piano in Orlando. Often she would entertain guests and neighbors with the songs of the day and with religious hymns. She also directed many other musical entertainments at the hotel located on Main Street, which was the hub of numerous social activities.

When Alice told her father that the congregation of the Episcopal Church, which she sometimes attended, was unable to sing hymns because of a lack of musical accompaniment, Jake bought a reed organ for the fledgling church. It was probably the first church organ in Orlando. Later the organ was placed in the courthouse, where it was more accessible to other congregations in the town. Fannie also enjoyed entertaining and was a charter member of the First Presbyterian Church of Orlando, which was founded in 1876.

Besides his business activities, Jake maintained a garden next to the hotel, and he often whiled away his rare moments of spare time by telling guests about his adventures during the Seminole Wars. He was never accused of being a braggart, but he developed a reputation of being a great storyteller. One reporter described him as a "great listener" because whenever he engaged in conversation, he gave his total attention to the one speaking.

One favorite Orlando anecdote about Jake reportedly occurred shortly after the Southern Railroad was completed. One day, a traveling salesman arrived from somewhere up North. After getting off the train, he called upon Jake to carry his valise to the Summerlin Hotel. Jake was dressed in his usual cowboy attire, and the drummer assumed he was an unemployed layabout who simply was trying to pick up some spare change. Jake told him he would carry his luggage for a quarter. The deal was settled, and Jake carried his valise to the hotel. The drummer did not find out until much later that his porter was one of the richest men in Florida.[13]

At times Summerlin seemed to enjoy playing the wag, especially around newspaper reporters. On a business trip to Tallahassee shortly after moving to

[12]*Ibid.*
[13]*Ibid.*

Orlando, the following item appeared in the *Weekly Floridian* on September 23, 1873:

> *Distinguished Visitor* – Mr. Jacob Summerlin, better known as "Old Jake," a distinguished citizen in South Florida, and the largest cattle owner in the world, arrived in this city this morning. He says he thinks more of a heifer calf than a male calf, "Seeing how they increase the stock faster." This is his peculiar theory on stock raising and he ought to know.
>
> Mr. Summerlin has a "theory" with a great deal of good sense in it. He says "the best investment a man can make is in a cow," that the stock of cattle in South Florida is yearly diminishing—and why? Because the stock owners are shipping off the she cattle instead of keeping them to renew supply. "My stock minders were doing this, but I have given strict orders, not another she critter shall be sold...[unless] she be done breeding." This is sensible and shows that "Uncle Jake's" head is level on the cattle question. He gave it as his opinion that 5,500 head are shipped monthly from Punta Rassa, Tampa and Manatee. This is a heavy drain and unless the idea...is observed...it will not take long for the demand to over-lap the supply.[14]

It appears in this interview that the reporter was also having fun and was a master of irony—an early Dave Barry.

In time, Jake became tired of the rather mundane role of hotelier. There had never been anything in his life that held as much appeal as the business of working cattle. Summerlin loved every phase of it from hunting, penning and branding to sales. It was a yearning, almost an addiction, that any cowman appreciated then and still appreciates today. He always felt more comfortable in the saddle astride his favorite one-man horse, *Morgan*. And the West Indian trade was booming again. It was said of Jake that "his field of operation was the entire Florida Peninsula and no pent-up Utica confines."

According to Dena Snodgrass, "He said to Bob Summerlin, to John Bigelow and to Sam one day as they were talking, 'I'm getting tired of this business of running this hotel—can't you boys take it off my hands?' The three jumped at the chance. Bigelow became general manager, Bob (just out of law school at Athens and needing contacts) stayed in the office and Sam 'just hung around a little while.'" But Sam liked the cattle business as much as his father did and, one day in 1875, he told him, "I want to work in the business." He soon left for St. Augustine where he acted there as Jake's cattle agent.

One of Summerlin's most significant land purchases was the acquisition of 200 acres of land from W.R. Lovell in 1875. This property was located in what for a long time was the very center of Orlando's business district and included Lake Eola—one of Orlando's most famous landmarks. The Summerlins gave

---

[14]"Distinguished Visitor," *Weekly Floridian*, 23 Sept. 1873, p. 3.

Lake Eola its present name, but there are two stories on why this name was chosen. One explanation was that Sam Summerlin named it for a girlfriend he had while attending school in Georgia. The other story was that Bob Summerlin, Sam's brother and then an attorney, named the lake for a sweetheart of his that had recently died from typhoid.

Jake built another large and elegant home on the south side of the lake. W.C. Stubblefield was the contractor. Later Jake donated part of the property to the town of Orlando, which included a strip, sixty feet wide all the way around the lake and specified that this piece of land had to be beautified and be made into a park. One reporter wrote later that this was the beginning of a long-running beautification movement that would one day entitle Orlando to be called "The City Beautiful." Orlando's incredible growth in later years can be attributed, in part, to its natural beauty, especially the lakes, and the willingness of many of its residents to maintain a pride in its near park like appearance.

At first, the city failed to maintain Lake Eola Park, and Jake threatened to repossess it. In 1883, the town council finally appropriated money for its care and even allocated funds for a white sand beach, a bathing house and a horse race track. Wallace Stevens of the *New York Times* wrote that Summerlin gave other strips of land around the many Orlando Lakes, for which Summerlin was recognized for establishing what became Orlando's system of public parks.[15]

In June 1875, the village of Orlando was incorporated as a town with a permanent population of over 200 people. A town council was elected, and Summerlin was appointed first president. Other aldermen included such familiar names as James Hughey, E.W. Speer, C.A. Boone, J.R. Cohen, J.W. Williams, W.C. Stubblefield and E.A. Richards. From 1876 to 1879, Robert "Bob" Summerlin, one of Jake's sons also served as an alderman, and in 1880, he was elected mayor. Eleven days after their first meeting, the town council convened in the new courthouse that had been financed by Jake. The late W.R. O'Neal, a columnist for the Orlando *Sentinel Star*, later wrote that Jacob Summerlin was easily the most outstanding man in Florida in 1867, and that in 1875, "Summerlin employed surveyors and grove owner J.J. Davis to lay off a plat which was to be known as Summerlins' addition to Orlando." Alma Hetherington wrote, "Jake was public spirited, but his donations were judicious and always in the public good."[16]

Of the significant contributions that Jake made toward the early growth and development of Orlando, none was more important than the role he played in establishing the town as the county seat. Orange County was carved out of

---

[15]Rick Brunson, "The King of the Crackers and O-Town, Jacob Summerlin and the Development of Orlando: 1873-1893." Paper presented at annual meeting of FHS at Cocoa, Florida: May 1998, p. 30; Akerman, "Jacob Summerlin," *Florida Pathfinders*, p. 123.

[16]W.R. O'Neal, "Memoirs," *Orlando Sentinel Star*, date missing, Bronson Papers.

Mosquito County in 1845. It was Florida's eleventh county and was named for the many orange groves in the area. In 1856 the unofficial county seat was located at Enterprise, or Fort Reed, which is now in Volusia County. The same year a "Log Court House" was built in Orlando and the center of county government was moved there. During the fall term of the Orange County Circuit Court, the courthouse was set afire. "Despite the efforts of bucket brigades from the town well, manned by men in their nightclothes, the log structure burned to the ground, destroying practically all county records." Another courthouse was built at the same location, but by the 1870s, it was no longer adequate to handle the business of a growing county.[17]

"Orlando thus was duly, by the selection of proper authorities, the seat of county government and the lawful location of the courthouse, yet it was scarcely more than a town and had prospects less bright in the ordinary eye, than have most country post offices of the county," wrote J. Holland Starbuck publisher for *The Democrat* of Orlando, "Yet to the eyes of Mr. Jacob Summerlin, the town had the brightest prospects."

General Henry S. Sanford, a former American Consul to Belgium, had recently moved to Mellonville. Sanford's military title came by way of an honorary commission from the State of Minnesota which he had acquired during the Civil War. In 1871, he purchased 12,000 acres of land that would later become a part of Seminole County. Soon after he planted citrus groves and began to provide the infrastructure for a large community. The age of the Florida developer was about to begin. Like Summerlin, Sanford built a large hotel that soon became very popular with visitors. It was located on Lake Monroe, a part of the St. Johns waterway, where side-wheelers and sternwheelers picked up citrus, timber and other goods to haul north. Sanford soon offered to build a courthouse for the people of Orange County if they would agree to move the county seat to Mellonville. The site had many advantages, particularly its location on Florida's most active waterway, the St. Johns River. The proposed move had the support of northern capitalists in the area.

General Sanford and Jake Summerlin appeared before the county commissioners in 1875 to make their appeals as to where the permanent county seat should be. Sanford painted a glowing picture of the beauty and potential of Mellonville. He was eloquent and forceful in his presentation, and even offered land and money if Mellonville became the county seat. The commissioners were almost persuaded to accept Sanford's offer and plan, but there was some concern that the town would lose its importance when the railroad reached Orlando.

After Sanford's persuasive presentation, Jake rose before the commissioners

---

[17]*Ibid.*; Allen and Joan Morris, "Orange County," *The Florida Handbook*. (Tallahassee: Peninsular Publishing, 2003-2004), p. 489; Shofner, *Orlando, The City Beautiful*, p. 34.

and stated in a quiet, calm voice, "I will make my offer. The county seat has its land for the courthouse here in Orlando. Leave this place the county seat and I will build a $10,000 courthouse, and if the county is ever able to pay for it, all right, and if not, I won't ask to be repaid."

This offer was quickly accepted by the commissioners and Orlando has been the county seat ever since. Commissioner Major Alexander St. Clair Abrams promised Jake he would be repaid if it took "all the land in the county."

Jake's son, Sam, later stated that Sinclair Abrauer (?) was responsible for the building of the courthouse, but the actual construction was completed by W.C. Stubblefield who had acquired an enviable reputation by this time as a building contractor. The "new" courthouse was a three-story wooden structure, and on the courtyard grounds, Summerlin insisted that a well be dug to supply water for the horses of patrons. It was 42 feet deep, lined with terra cotta and protected by a well house with a shingled roof. The courthouse served Orlando until 1892 when Orange County's growing population required a new and larger one. Later Summerlin's 1875 courthouse was moved to Church and Main Streets and became a part of the Tremont Hotel.

When court was in session, the community took on almost a festive atmosphere. Covered wagons and tents surrounded the courthouse as families from all over the county descended upon the little town. A wispy smoke haze hung in the air left over from the small fires used to prepare meals on the ground. Odors from fried bacon, camp coffee and beans drifted across the town into the corridors of the courthouse and the nearby homes. Children were everywhere, left on their own while the adults tended to business.[18]

One day while she was visiting Mrs. Kina Fries, Fannie Summerlin made a rather astute observation of Orlando's unrestricted growth, "I sit here and see to the east orange trees cut down, farther out, the pine trees crashing to the ground, houses facing a street where travelers rush by." Even then, she could see the great attraction Orlando had and recognized how ungracefully the town would grow into a city.

---

[18]Louise Frisbie, "Pioneers," Parts 9 and 10, *The Democrat and Leader*, November, 1973; E.H. Gore, *From Florida Sand to "The City Beautiful:" A Historical Record of Orlando, Florida* (Orlando, 1951); Akerman, "Jacob Summerlin," *Florida Pathfinders* pp. 122-123; Gene Burnett, "Florida's Cattleman Monarch," *Florida Trend*, November 1977, p. 105; Baynard H. Kendrick, *Orlando-A Century Plus*. (Orlando Sentinel Star Co., 1976), p. 16.

Chapter 8

Summerlin's Years at Punta Rassa

One of the oldest Spanish place names in Florida was Punta Rassa, or "Level Point" in English, which was given to a tiny wind swept spit of land at the Fort Myers end of what is now the Sanibel Causeway. Before the Spanish gave it their name, however, a camp of Calusa Indians lived there. They called it "Point of Swift Waters." Both names aptly described the geography of this locale. Once the refuge of pirates, a U.S. marine garrison during the Indian Wars, a vital communication link between Florida and Cuba and an excellent port for the exportation of cracker cattle, the importance of this site has been lost to modern residents and is covered today with high-rise apartments and other residences. The modern city of Fort Myers is much better known. Patricia Bartlett, the former director of the Fort Myers Historical Museum, summed up the early history of the two towns with a simple statement. "For a long time Fort Myers was merely a freckle on the face of the earth, and Punta Rassa was the far more important of the two."[1]

In 1864, Union soldiers stationed at Fort Myers, an old Indian fort, built a wharf at Punta Rassa for loading the cattle they had stolen or bought from Florida settlers in the interior. Most of these cows were loaded on small ships and taken to Key West, a town controlled by Union forces throughout the Civil War.

Summerlin knew the area well since he had hunted and driven cattle in the region and had served as a scout for Major Footman's force in 1865. He knew its potential. By 1866, the area was almost deserted, but even that year approximately 1,600 head of cattle had been shipped from there to Cuba. Some of these beeves belonged to Summerlin.

In order to stimulate development of modern communications, Congress passed legislation in the late 1860s allowing telegraph companies the right to take and use public lands necessary for the stringing of wires or the establish-

---

[1]Patricia Bartlett, personal interview, Fort Myers, FL: May 1994; Akerman, "Jacob Summerlin," *Florida Pathfinders* p. 123; Julia Pate, "Punta Rassa, Part 1-500 B.C. to 1886," Fort Myers Historical Society, Fort Myers, March/April 1984.

ment of needed relay stations. It was still all part of the movement known as "manifest destiny," which was directed toward American territorial, political and commercial expansion. In 1867, Punta Rassa was selected as the site for the terminus of the International Ocean and Telegraph Company (IOTC) line, which ran under water from Punta Rassa to Key West and then underwater again to Havana, Cuba. Cattle trades were often made using this line, thus facilitating trade with Cuba, Key West, Duval County, Fort Meade and other points where cattle were needed or could be collected. A small Union barracks had been built on pilings at the port and remained deserted after the end of the war. The IOTC built a 100-foot by 50-foot barracks to house employees and to serve as an office. During the 1873 hurricane, the barracks built by the IOTC served as a refuge for the few settlers who lived nearby. Eventually the IOTC was bought out by Western Union.[2]

Captain F.A. Hendry, a close friend of Summerlin's, built another wharf at Punta Rassa in 1870. It was much larger and stronger than the one built during the Civil War, and it included holding pens and other facilities. Jake and his son, Sam, used the wharf for shipping cattle to Cuba, and in the fall of 1878, Jake purchased the wharf and existing facilities from Hendry for $10,000. A reporter from the *Sunland Tribune* of Tampa wrote after the sale, "Uncle Jake is determined to control the entire shipping business of the Caloosahatchee region." That same year Jake and Sam moved to Punta Rassa.[3]

To help insure a constant supply of beeves for sale, Jake, Sam and their drovers moved a herd of 3,000 cattle into the lower Fisheating Creek area. Part of this herd, known as the C-5 herd, was sold later directly to Captain John Whidden.[4] Soon after the Whidden sale, the Summerlins became partners with Bill Towles of Fort Myers and Taylor County for a brief time. Towles and Summerlin jointly owned a large cattle herd, which they moved to an ungrazed range southeast of old Fort Thompson and across the Oklaochoobee Slough. Ironically, Oklaochoobee means "bad luck" or "no good" in Mikasuki, but it became good luck to Summerlin and Towles since it formed a natural fence for the cattle and kept them from wandering into the Everglades where they would become wild as deer. But as more and more cows drifted into the Glades, Summerlin and Towles decided to erect a real fence from a point twelve miles east of present day LaBelle to a point on the east side of Oklaochoobee Slough. It was seventeen miles long. Although free range was still

[2]Brown, *Florida's Peace River Frontier*, pp. 217-219. Brown points out that Peace River residents involved with the Tampa and Fort Meade Telegraph Co. were James T. Wilson, Philip Dzialynski, Frederick Varn, John Skipper and Charles L. Mitchell, p. 410, note 10; Canter Brown, *Jewish Pioneers of the Tampa Bay Frontier*. (Tampa: Tampa Bay History Center Reference Library, 1999), p. 55; Julia Pate, *Ibid.* p. 47.

[3]Bronson Papers.

[4]VanLandingham and Akerman, "Florida's Early Cattle Kings," unpublished manuscript.

an enshrined concept among Florida cattle ranchers, the fence was built to keep their cattle from straying away from their pasture, not to keep other cattle off the range. It was an unusual fence built by a man named Sam Lucky. Lucky made the posts and poles from heart pine using forty-penny spikes to attach the poles to the posts. Barbed wire, which had been invented by Joseph Glidden of Illinois in 1873, was not widely employed at this time and was not part of the original fence. Later, however, ribbon wire was later added above two lines of poles of the new fence. The fence was so exceptional that it was given a name, "the Summerlin-Towles-Lucky fence." According to Albert Devane, "The success of this fence, as viewed by other cattlemen, was cause for a similar fence to be built by James Hendry and 'Doc' Langford of Fort Myers. It was built by a man named Clinton Curry who used Indian labor along with their cowboys."[5]

Soon after his purchase of Hendry's wharf at Punta Rassa, Jake decided to expand the existing facilities by constructing a building for his home and a hotel to accommodate drovers, cowboys, ranchers and Spanish cattle buyers from Cuba and other visitors. Hunters, journalists and those curious to meet the "King of the Crackers" often came by. The Punta Rassa boarding house was not as elegant as his hotel in Orlando, but perhaps, it better reflected the character of the man. It was a solid edifice and the rustic furnishings served Jake and his boarders and visitors just fine.

What made this simple, spacious dwelling so different from other lodgings in the area were the shiny, fat yellow Spanish doubloons that were often piled on tables or bundled into corn sacks and thrown into corners. The coins were not guarded. Although the Summerlins "knew some men [that were] mean enough to steal cows and put on them the wrong brand, who would be mean enough to steal dollars and cents?" Many cattlemen in Florida handled Spanish money in a similar manner, but there were few complaints made to lawmen about the theft of gold doubloons.[6]

Besides the wharf and other facilities, Jake also bought 1,000 acres of land for holding cattle. Sometimes the pens were almost completely filled as beeves destined for the West Indies milled about, waiting to be loaded on ships. Americans, such as Captain McKay, Bill Towles and Dr. H.T. Lykes, owned most of the ships, but Cuban ships, such as the *Guillermo*, were sometimes used. A few Spanish cattle agents lived in Fort Myers for part of the year. Other Spanish agents lived in Tampa, where many cracker cattle were loaded at Ballast Point.

---

[5]Joe Akerman, "Open Range and Fencing in Early Florida," *The Florida Cattleman*, January 2004, pp. 20-21.

[6]Lisa Gentzler, "Punta Rassa Not Immune to Development," *News Press/Acey Harper*, 1974; Akerman, *Florida Cowman*, p. 159; Mr. and Mrs. Gerard Kinzie, "History of Punta Rassa." Southwest Florida Historical Society. D.B. McKay, "Lived Like a Pauper," *Tampa Tribune*, date missing. Bronson Papers.

Jacob Summerlin

Summerlin allowed other cattle exporters to use his pens and wharf at Punta Rassa for a small fee. The number of cattle that passed through this port is difficult to determine, but some sense of the magnitude of the operation can be gathered from the remarks of Theron Moore, a modern day contractor who developed the site for apartments, "The woods for miles around gave off the pungent odor of cow manure where thousands of cattle must have been once penned. And no matter how deep we dug we still encountered the manure. Some of that cow dung must have come from some of old Jake Summerlin's cows. That smell suddenly brought us way back in time."[7]

Other wharves were built at Fort Ogden, Cedar Key, Panama River, along the Manatee River and at Hickory Bluff, but none were so convenient and negotiable as those at Punta Rassa and Tampa, despite the fact that cattle sometimes had to be driven from great distances. Some cows were herded all the way from South Georgia. On these long drives, cattle were usually allowed to graze for two hours in early morning before they were headed out at sunrise. At noon the cowmen usually stopped long enough for the "cookie" to make coffee. But this was only a short respite, and Jake said he often finished his coffee while in the saddle. Late in the afternoon the cows were allowed to graze for two more hours. It was important that they not lose too much weight before reaching their destination. At night the cattle were usually driven into pens. If the cowmen were lucky and skilled at working cattle, they reached these pens about dusk, but, of course, there were a thousand things that could go wrong, not the least of which was a stampede. The cows "were as wild as buffalo to begin with, and a crack of thunder or the howl of wolves or panthers on the outer perimeter could turn a herd into an earthquake of hoofs." Cowman "Teet" Holmes of St. Lucie County said that a stampede of beeves at night could slow up a cattle drive for a whole day. He added, "high water and flooded rivers and creeks could slow up a drive for days."[8]

A major problem for cattle owners was timing the arrival of their herds at the port since the Spanish buyers at Punta Rassa often set deadlines for the delivery of cattle. Driving cattle from North Florida to Punta Rassa sometimes took from forty to sixty days, a task made more difficult by Florida's unpredictable weather and the behavior of wild cattle. Often Spanish buyers would fine Summerlin and his associates if they failed to meet a contracted deadline. On one occasion, the Summerlins had a contract with a Don Pedro de la Noval to deliver 1,200 head of cattle at $10.00 per head, a price that would be good only if the cows were delivered on time. The Summerlins and their associates agreed

[7]Theron Moore, personal Interview, Madison, May 1999; Akerman, *Florida Cowman*, p. 285.
[8]Nathan Holmes personal Interview, Fort Pierce, 22 December 1975; Akerman, *Florida Cowman*, pp. 150-151, 165-166, 176, 185, 229, 241.

to pay a penalty of $1,000 for each day late if they failed to deliver on time. Unfortunately one week before the delivery date, heavy rains inundated the Caloosahatchee River Valley, and the normally placid river was turned into a raging torrent of muddy water. In some places, it was over a mile wide. Making a raft from cabbage logs, the resourceful cowboys, using poles, pushed the crude boat, loaded with cows, upstream on the edges of the currents until they reached some cattle pens that were above water. The first cattle were driven into the large holding pens just before the deadline; so they received the full account promised by the *hidalgo*. By the time they were able to round up the remainder of the cattle and drive them across the flooded plain, the river had receded and they were able to herd the cows on to Punta Rassa.

Spanish captains who came to Punta Rassa from Cuba with their golden doubloons regarded Jake as a "man who couldn't be cheated, who wouldn't gamble and who never drank."[9] Perhaps their admiration for him also stemmed from his calm manner and his plain attire. His cotton trousers and shirt, his leather boots and a five-gallon hat puzzled and disarmed them—to be so rich and so revered and yet to dress like the Cuban *canaille*. It was said that when the bright coins tumbled out on the table for counting, his eyes never flickered.[10] He was little impressed with wealth, but he had a deep appreciation for the practical wisdom and hard work it took to acquire it.

There were many stories concerning Jake's gold. Typical of these concerned a cattle buying trip in Volusia County when he rode up to a rather rundown inn to eat and to have his horse fed and rubbed down. When he dismounted, he threw his saddlebags, which contained about $6,000 in Spanish doubloons, over his shoulders. "He was dressed for the range and wore no coat, the most conspicuous article of dress being a bandana looped over his neck." After he had eaten and asked the hostess about his charges, she replied, "Poor old man; you seem to be having a hard time. You may give me 25 cents if you have it." He ended up giving her ten dollars in gold and several gold pieces to her children.[11]

Summerlin's drovers were soon buying cattle over most of the state and herding most of them to Punta Rassa. Sometimes they would buy only a few cattle from a farmer or, on other occasions, they would collect fifty or a hundred head from large pens where they were being held for Summerlin's cowmen or other

---

[9]*Ibid.*, p. 124; D.B. McKay, "Lived Like a Pauper," Tampa *Tribune*, date missing. Bronson Papers; "King of the Crackers," *Florida Times Union*, 25 Sept. 1883.

[10]Historical notes owned by Florida Cattlemen's Association, Kissimmee; D.B. McKay, "Lived Like a Pauper," Tampa *Tribune*, date missing. Bronson Papers; Akerman, *Florida Cowman*, pp. 113-114.

[11]Wallace Stevens, "Cattle Kings of Florida," Atlanta *Journal*. Atlanta, 14 Dec. 1930, p. 1; Louise Frisbie, "A Surprise Guest," *The Democrat and Leader*, 20 Nov. 1973.

cowmen who rode for the Laniers, the Aldermans, the Parkers, the Hendrys and others. It was an exciting time to be a drover. Cowmen usually paid four to six dollars per head, depending on the age, the confirmation and the weight of the cows. They often would pay in scrip issued by Summerlin or other affluent cattlemen, or sometimes in paper currency and often in Spanish doubloons. At times, Summerlin would ride with his drovers and give sellers his I.O.U.s.[12]

There were cattle trails over all of the state. One of Summerlin's favorite routes to Punta Rassa was along what was called the Wire Road, which turned southeastward below Brooksville to Fort Meade, went on to Fort Thompson at the Caloosahatchee River and ran westward to Fort Myers. At Fort Myers, Jake's cowboys had to push the cattle across a saltwater slough about 600 yards wide. It was very boggy and in some places the bottom was quicksand. Cowmen usually cut fifteen-foot logs from old pines about ten to twelve inches square, which they used to build a rough road across the slough. Most of the cattle were made to swim across the Caloosahatchee River. This was the tricky part of the operation. The cattle didn't like to swim perpendicular to the flow of the river. By using a 10' x 18' scow that was rowed across the river at an angle, the current of the river was disrupted and the cattle swam with the waves made by the scow. Cow ponies were also carried over on the scow. It was a slow process, but Sam Summerlin remembered driving 3,000 head over on one drive.[13]

One of the cattle trails used most often by the Summerlins began at Sanchez's pens near St. Augustine. One of them, usually Sam, would enter the pens on a particular date and select those cattle he wanted to buy. If the payment, which often ranged from five to ten dollars a head, was satisfactory to Sanchez, Spanish gold coins were used to pay him on the spot. Sometimes Sam or Jake might give the seller an I.O.U. or, when Florida's banks were more established, he might even use a check. Then the drovers would herd the cattle southward, frequently adding more stock before reaching Punta Rassa.

From St. Augustine, the first important stop was Braddock's large pens near Harve Creek in the western part of Volusia County. Braddock and his neighbors would usually have their pens full of cattle by the time the drovers approached the pens. From Harve Creek, the cattle were driven southwestward to Holden Prairie, a rich green river bottom located on the St. Johns River between Cook's Ferry and Lake Monroe. The Osteens, the Yates, the Johnsons, the Smiths, the Tuckers, the Woodruffs and the Howards were some of the families who penned cattle for the drovers. By the time the herd left Holden Prairie, it usually contained about 500 or 600 head. From there, the herd would move

---

[12]Akerman, *Florida Cowman*, pp. 55-56, 85-86, 101, 104, 168.

[13]Crow, "Cattle Drives," *Osceola Sun*, 17 June 1976; Cecil Tucker, II, "Indian Paths, Military Roads, and the Cattle Trails of Florida," *Florida Cattle Frontier Symposium: 1845-1995*, pp. 135-139.

across the St. Johns River. Local cattle were used as leaders when crossing wide creeks and rivers and once they started to swim, the other cattle usually followed. Drovers used their whips to drive any laggards. Crossing the St. Johns was dangerous and occasionally "a few of the cows became exhausted if the river was high and wide, and they would drown. Sometimes the river was 300 yards across."[14]

Just west of the St. Johns, near present day Geneva, the Hart family also kept large pens. Further south, the concentration pens for the Orlando area were located just east of Lake Conway. This was near the Dave Mizell home place. While this was probably the largest single area for assembling cows on this trail, one reporter obviously exaggerated when he said he saw 167,000 head there in the 1880s. Following the Old Fort Brook-Fort Mellon Trail, the Summerlins and their crew crossed Shingle Creek and picked up the old Jessup Trail on their way to Bonnet Creek. And from there, they pushed the cattle down the so-called Secret Indian Trail. This was a particularly risky area because it was heavily wooded and thick with scrub. The cry of a panther or the rumble of thunder might cause a herd to break into a hundred directions. Passing along the Secret Indian Trail, the route ran along the south end of Lake Tohopehaligo to Bill Shiver's scrub pens, located at the mouth of the Canoe Creek. The next stop was Captain Abner Johnson's pens near present day Whittier. A side trail, the Tiger Tail Trail, said to be made by a Seminole Chief, was used by some cowmen to drive cattle into Whittier. After leaving the Whittier area, the cowmen headed southeast to make contact with cattlemen out of Fort Drum. Swinging southwestward again, they crossed the Kissimmee River and bought more cows at Fort Basinger, now in Highlands County. Below Fort Basinger, the cattlemen were close enough to Summerlin's pens at Punta Rassa to herd their own cattle. Sometimes, though, they would drive their cows to Fort Pierce where there was another port.[15]

Drovers and cattlemen buying cattle were always faced with paying for them with some form of money that was acceptable to the owner of the cows. The lack of banks in Florida made this difficult and, since there were no banks south of Palatka before the 1880s, no commonly acceptable currency existed. Even United States currency was in a limited supply. A reporter for the Savannah *Morning News* visited south Florida in 1879 and described the use of "pernicious foreign gold and silver coins" to pay for cattle, "Doubloons were worth anywhere from fifteen to sixteen dollars, as the party traded with might be inclined to give. With a few doubloons and foreign silver dollars in pocket, one could experience Wall Street stock speculation in passing from town to town or dealer to dealer in the same town." Mexican dollars might be worth at eighty-five

---

[14]*Ibid.*
[15]Crow, *Old Tales and Trails of Florida*, pp. 57, 60, 138.

cents at one place , but worth only eighty cents at a store across the street. "At one place in the same town (in Florida) doubloons were worth fifteen dollars and fifty cents, at another fifteen dollars and thirty-five cents, and at another fifteen dollars. Each dealer said he was governed by the returns from his last shipment. The United States coins, on the other hand, were usually seen in dimes." The reporter described one cattle purchase for over a thousand dollars that was paid entirely in United States dimes.[16]

In dealings between cattlemen and even Spanish buyers, a verbal agreement was all that was necessary in transferring the ownership of cattle between two parties during those early years. "Honesty was abroad in the land and the word of a reliable person was the same as a contract." Summerlin himself described the transaction between buyer and seller in these words:

> The buyer approaches Mr. X, "Say, Mr. X, I'll pay you $10 per head and take all the steers three years old and up. You are to furnish one man to help drive the cattle to the Caloosahatchee River. There the cattle will be counted. If there are any short, we will report back to you. You look out for my interest if they ever come back on your range. Aside from that, I want you to put your inspector with the cattle so that no strays will be picked up on the road."
>
> There was no dispute over quantity. When the appointed day came, the buyer was on the ground with his saddlebags of Spanish gold. The cattle were inspected and the buyer rejected anything that did not fill the bill.[17]

Although Florida cattlemen had been exporting cattle to the Spanish since the mid-1850s, the number sold up to the end of the Civil War was rather small. Conditions in Cuba created greater demands after 1868. Between 1868 and 1878, Cuban patriots, led by Carlos Manuel Cespedes, began a desperate struggle against Spanish authorities. A slave revolt had taken place earlier in 1812, but the Ten Year War (1868-1878) was a war for Cuban independence. As Cuban patriots began to seize land and livestock from the Spanish landowners, authorities began to look toward Florida as a source for replacement beef. Summerlin and F.A. Hendry began shipping cattle from Punta Rassa on Captain James McKay's ship the *Emily* in 1866, but initial profits were small. By 1868, however, buyers from Havana and even Key West were eager "to buy the small lean beeves at a range of $12.00 to $22.00 per head F.O.B."

Summerlin hired every drover he could find to hunt wild cattle and to buy the *criollo* or cracker cattle. Reporters and local historians have expressed differ-

---

[16]Louise Frisbie, "About Those Gold Doubloons," *The Polk County Democrat*, 15 Nov. 1973, Part 12; D.B. McKay, "Second Seminole War," *Pioneer Florida*, Vol. II, (Tampa: Southern Publishing Co., 1959), pp. 325-327.

[17]VanLandingham and Akerman, "Florida's Early Cattle Kings", p. 38.

ing impressions of what these drovers or "cracker cowboys" were like. Frank L. Owsley described them simply as "plain folks." Oliver O. Howard, a fervent Methodist, believed crackers to be as a "general thing, a very corrupt set of men." They drank, gambled, and swore and did all sorts of disreputable things. But to Ossian Hart, who became governor of Florida in 1873, cracker cowmen were larger than life heroes, who "roamed the woods for weeks and months on end, camping in the wilderness, independent of spirit...They communicated a lust for life and a deep affection for Florida's natural environment because many of them were more content with their lives, however miserable they may have appeared to others." Their character and customs appeared little different from those of western cowboys. "The older people are utterly wrapped up in the cattle business, and can conceive of no greater happiness to a dying mortal than to take the last expiring breath holding a cow whip in one hand and a cow's tail in the other."[18] Ossian Hart was probably thinking of his close friend Jake Summerlin when he expressed these thoughts.

Between 1870 and 1880, over 165,000 head of cattle were shipped to Cuba. Florida still suffered from a postwar depression and cattlemen were among the few Floridians making money. Their commerce stimulated the shipping businesses and promoted the growth of towns, such as Fort Myers, Orlando, Tampa and Kissimmee.[19]

The year 1879 was a particularly profitable one for cracker cattlemen. That year, Jake and Sam Summerlin sold 10,000 head, all for Spanish gold. During that same time, Captain William Hooker sold 12,000 cattle to Cuba; John T. Leslie sold 12,000 cattle; and F.A. Hendry sold 5,000. By 1880, Jake Summerlin reportedly owned or controlled all the cattle shipping from Fort Myers to Hickory Bluff.[20]

Jake and Sam Summerlin were among the first Florida cattlemen to rent range lands in Cuba. By 1878, there were few cows in Cuba with the exception of milch cows. Spanish soldiers and Cuban *insurrectos* consumed local cows to the point of extinction. The great abundance of rich range grasses on the island attracted the attention of the Summerlins, F.A. Hendry and other large time Florida cattlemen, who saw an advantage in bringing Florida scrub cattle into Cuba and fattening them up before sales. It didn't take long to put pounds on lean scrub cows because of Cuba's native grasses. Captain F.A. Hendry was so impressed with the Cuban pasturage that he planted Cuban grasses on his fenced range east of Fort Myers. It was one of the first attempts in Florida to establish "improved pasture" on a large scale.

---

[18]Brown, *Florida's Peace River Frontier*, pp. 24-25, 74-75.

[19]Karl Grismer, *The Story of Fort Myers*. (St. Petersburg: St. Petersburg Printing Co., 1949), pp. 79-82.

[20]VanLandingham and Akerman, "Florida's Early Cattle Kings", p. 112.

Summerlin never revealed his thoughts about Cuba, especially Havana, which was founded in 1519 and was already an old city by New World standards. Not unlike modern Havana, it was a striking mixture of Mediterranean refinement and unrelenting squalor. It was the largest city in the West Indies, with a large natural harbor, many wide boulevards, imposing government buildings and baroque churches. Summerlin had visited Charleston, Savannah and, of course, St. Augustine, but it is doubtful that he had ever witnessed such uninhibited gaiety and ribaldry as he saw in Havana despite the presence of large numbers of Spanish soldiers and police. Even the rebellion did little to dampen the spirits of the city's residents.

The Summerlins first leased land on a plantation in the vicinity of Nuevitas, in the Camaguey province. They "hired many Cubans to take care of the herds," which they drove from the landing at Nuevitas to the nearby ranges. Although Nuevitas was one of the Cuban ports nearest Punta Rassa, landing cows there proved to be very difficult. The only available wharf was approximately two hundred feet square with no outside railing and had been originally built for handling sugarcane products. When cattle were unloaded, Cubans were placed around the edges of the wharf, but this human fence did little to contain bunches of fifty or seventy-five wild woods cows that had not eaten or had water in several days. The frantic cows were virtually unmanageable and "sometimes they became frightened and jumped off into the water which was fifteen feet deep, and disappeared in rolling waves of the sea." Those that reached shore had trouble finding a place to climb out since the shore was lined with warehouses. Cuban *vaqueros*, using rowboats, directed the frightened cows to spots where they could reach land.

Twenty-five or thirty horsemen drove the cattle to the range where they were put out to pasture. The thirsty herds were split into small bunches and taken to water holes, but allowed "to drink a small amount of water because if they got their fill, it many times meant death. It was a terrible battle to get them away from the water." When they were driven onto the range, they completely disappeared in the tall grass in fifteen minutes or less. "There was little danger of them overeating because they were tired."[21]

From 1878 to 1882, cattle boats continued to cross the ocean from Florida to Cuba in an almost endless progression. A great number of the cattle went to Spanish soldiers stationed in Cuba. Cattlemen and shippers did extremely well with their Cuban trade, but in 1883, Spanish authorities placed a high tariff on imported beef in order to raise money for the army. The Cuban rebels had won some concessions from the Spanish government during the Ten Year War, but it appeared to the Spanish that another outbreak was on the horizon. The next

---

[21]Crow, "Cuban Trade," *Osceola* Sun, 15 July 1976; Brown, "Peace River Frontier Agriculture," unpublished manuscript, pp. 186-187.

revolt began in 1895.

Jake had died in 1893, but his sons contiued to export beeves by the thousands and those they did not sell on the spot in Havana or Sagua La Grande, they placed on the Nuevitas range. Soon they had a herd of a thousand or more there. When the Spanish government appointed General William "Butcher" Weyler as governor of the island and instructed him to stop the rebellion, Jake had been dead several years, but Sam carried on the Nuevitas operation for a while. In 1896, custodians of his cattle herd informed him that it was impossible for them to protect his stock any longer because of the insurrection. "The Spanish soldiers would cut the fence on one side and take his cattle, and the Cubans would do likewise on the opposite side which rendered them powerless against the situation."[22]

The Cuban market was fairly dependable until after World War I, but some fluctuations occurred. When the Cuban trade was unsteady or not so profitable, the Summerlins and other Florida cattlemen turned to domestic markets to sell their cattle, especially after railroads began to cross Central and South Florida. There was always a dependable market in Key West for ships loaded with cattle and Punta Rassa and Tampa would remained the major ports for this trade.[23]

A.H. Curtiss, a reporter for the *Florida Dispatch*, gave the following description of Punta Rassa or "Summerlin Port" in the 1880s:

Long before we came in sight of the wharf we could see the roofs of the upper works of a steamer, which proved to be the *Guillielerrmo* awaiting a load of cattle for Cuba. About sunset we came abreast of the great steamer, and a little beyond to anchor. The *Guillielerrmo* was painted black with stripes of red—this and the rough-jargon of the Spanish crew made her seem just a little piratical.

On shore there was a bedlam of sounds, the bellowing of penned cattle, the cries of drovers, the barking of dogs, the cracking of whips—sometimes eighteen feet in length with a short handle. The cowboys are very expert in using and cracking it and have acquired the sobriquet of "crackers." As night drew on the noise increased. Bonfires and torches flared in the darkness. Bellowing herds came pouring in from the back woods, until at nine o'clock five hundred cattle were ready to be transferred to the steamer. From the cattleyard to the steamer extended a long and narrow passageway, boarded on the sides, through which the cattle were driven. A dozen at a time were started, then with loud cries, blows and clatter of hoofs cattle and drivers came rushing down to the steamer. These cattle were huddled together and penned by themselves; this process was continued until late at night. We went to sleep

---

[22]*Ibid.*, 29 July 1976.

[23]Akerman, *Florida Cowman*, pp. 119-120; "Cuban Market," *Desota County News*, 15 Sept. 1905.

in pandemonium, as it seemed, but when we awoke all was serene and quiet. Early in the morning...the *Guillielerrmo* got up steam and there was a hurrying to and fro with papers and parcels to do what had been forgotten 'till the last moment. When the scene recurs to me, I see two olive-skinned sailor boys, with flowing black hair and gleaming white teeth and eyes constantly sparkling with mirth as if their lives overflowed with happiness...then only a few months later the *Guillielerrmo* was overwhelmed by a hurricane and sank with all aboard.

Soon after the departure...another smaller schooner came in to load cattle. Thus the business goes on [and] Mr. Jake Summerlin usually attends to the transfer. There is no need for a town here, and there is none."[24]

Curtiss wondered why anyone would live on such a desolate, sandy cape by choice, "Yet here in the desert-like place, in that ugly old building, with the bare necessities of life around him, lives one of the richest men in Florida, who could, if he would, live in princely style anywhere in the state. But Jacob Summerlin had not the spirit of a nabob."

Jake had experienced poverty as a younger man. Although wealthy now, he retained the personal habits of the impoverished and "has ever been the poor man's friend and protector." He seemed to have a perfect indifference to anything more than necessities. Curtiss remarked, "I could not realize that the little old man whom I found...cutting up a slaughtered beef was the 'King of the Crackers,' whose name is known throughout Florida and Cuba."[25] According to his service record from the Second Seminole War, Summerlin was not so small and was listed at 5'8" and 5'9" tall. Perhaps it was the way he dressed and the slight stoop he had when he was 60 years old that caused Curtiss to deem him as "little." Photographs made of Jake in the 1880s do not suggest that he was small.

Curtiss was one of the reporters that recognized how curious Summerlin was about so many things. When they talked on the front porch of his large bunkhouse, Curtiss soon recognized what a fertile mind Jake had. Curtiss "showed him a heavy, odd-shaped vertebra of an extinct seal (*Phocodon*)," which he had found on the shore close by. Jake told him of a curious feed-box which he used before the Civil War, a picket joint of a mastodon, which he could use to hold a peck of oats for feeding his horses. He blamed Union soldiers for stealing it.

An article that appeared in the New York *Daily Tribune*, September 16, 1883, informed readers that Summerlin's nickname, "King of the Crackers," was one that "mightily pleased him. Because he was proud of the early dangers he faced and the

---

[24]D.B. McKay, "Lived Like a Pauper," Tampa *Tribune*; Akerman, "Jacob Summerlin and Florida's Early Cattle Industry," Program given at Madison County Historical Society, Madison, 1 May 1999; "Letter From Manatee," The Savannah *Morning News*, 3 August 1875.

[25]D.B. McKay, "Pioneer Florida," Tampa *Tribune*. "Punta Rassa," Savannah *Morning News*, 15 July 1880, p. 1.

experiences of growing up on the frontier; he dreams, lives, talks and trades as a poor man might, but he gives to the poor and defends the cause of the fatherless against the land shark as only a rich man can...He wears a checkered homespun shirt, old blue trousers and stockman boots or shoes. He plowed his own garden and watered his own mule in 'ostentatious humility.'" But these were the things a "cracker" should be, and he was prouder of that title, "King of the Crackers" than all the wealth he had. He said once, "I don't want anymore clothes than those I have, my boys can dress up in store clothes, if it suits 'em — go to college — talk big. I'm going on this way 'till I drop in my tracks." [26]

During the years that Jake lived at Punta Rassa, he hired several full-time cooks for his boarding house. He kept over 100 chickens, so there would always be fresh eggs for his guests. The hotel soon developed a reputation for having an excellent cracker cuisine that included fresh venison, beef and mullet, as well as the fresh vegetables he raised. A Savannah journalist, who visited Punta Rassa on July 4, 1880, bragged about the cheer and hospitality of "Colonel" Summerlin. He described his stay there as the return of "the good old feeling of ante-bellum days."[27] That same year, a fellow cattleman, Captain John M. Pearce, took a party to Summerlin's Punta Rassa hotel for dinner. Pearce wrote, "there was much good food to eat, but no drink since Summerlin was a prohibitionist."[28]

Despite the activity at Punta Rassa and his full working days, he missed his family. Sam was away most of the time buying and driving cattle. Jasper, whom he saw only occasionally, had a large cattle operation in Manatee County with over 5,000 head of stock. Gideon had a cattle operation in Polk County. Robert, George, Alice, and Martha, or "Mollie," were all married and lived in Central Florida. The one person he missed the most was Fannie, his wife, who was living in Orlando and had practically become a "cattleman's widow." She had decided against going to Punta Rassa because Orlando apparently agreed with her health. At times, Jake would mount up *Old Morgan* and make the long ride to Orlando to be with Fannie and to take care of business matters.

Sam Summerlin, who stayed at Punta Rassa when he was not on the trail or in Cuba, developed a particular closeness with his father. Jake had taken him along on business trips or cattle drives as soon as he was old enough to ride a horse, and he grew to love every phase of the cattle business just as much as Jake did. When he was still in his teens, he had developed a proficiency in keeping books, and more and more, Jake turned this function over to him. After 1879, he kept all the books at Punta Rassa — certainly not an easy task by this time.[29]

---

[26]*New York Daily Tribune*, 16 Sept. 1883, p. 1; Gene Burnett, "Florida's Cattleman Monarch," *Florida Trend*, November 1977, p. 105.

[27]Letter from Cedar Keys," Savannah *Morning News*, 15 July 1880, p. 1.

[28]"Letter from Visitor," Tampa *Guardian*, 14 Aug. 1880, p. 2.

[29]Crow, *Old Tales and Trails of Florida*, p. 53.

Prince Johnson, once a slave of Jake Summerlin, stayed with Summerlin several years after the end of the Civil War but later applied for a homestead in Polk County in 1871. Johnson received 80 acres on which he established a successful farming operation. He and his wife reared six children on this farm and were able to send several to school.

Chapter 9

Connecting the Caloosahatchee

When the Democrats regained political control of Florida in 1876, the state embarked on several new economic and political directions. Although racial attitudes had changed little since antebellum times, the so-called "Bourbons"[1] encouraged new internal developments and increased commerce for the state.

Taking a page from Henry Clay's American System, the Democrats adopted a platform which advocated "a liberal policy on the matter of public improvements, and held that the South has a right to demand this until her waterways and harbors have been adjusted to the needs of commerce to the extent as in other sections of the country."[2] African-American Republicans serving in the State Legislature also supported this policy. It is a political blueprint that most Florida governors and legislatures have more or less supported ever since.

Areas targeted by the legislature for development included Central and South Florida, particularly the land and water systems between the headwaters of the St. Johns south to Lake Okeechobee and westward to the Gulf of Mexico. This area was particularly important to the cattlemen, and they were well represented in the legislature. In 1879, Senator F.A. Hendry and several other men of influence asked the old scout, Jacob Summerlin, to guide a survey party from Fort Myers to the headwaters of the Caloosahatchee River to determine the most appropriate route for a canal that would join the Caloosahatchee to Lake Okeechobee, thus creating a direct link from Kissimmee and Central Florida to the Gulf of Mexico. Who was better qualified than Jake to lead this survey? He knew the territory so well. He had been offered a role in the development of Peas Creek (Peace River) back in 1866.

---

[1] The name "Bourbon" as it applied to the southern white Democrats, presumably referred to the French Bourbon monarchy which had forgotten nothing and learned nothing; however, this was in part a misnomer because the postwar southern Democrats were committed to industrial and population growth and success with these goals required internal improvements, particularly in the area of transportation—new roads, improved waterways, railroads and canals.

[2] Tebeau, *A History of Florida*, pp. 258-272.

Jake wrote to the *Sunland Tribune* in June 1880, "I received several communications from parties insisting very hard on my meeting them and their steamboat there (Fort Myers) on the 13th and 15th of January."[3] The parties he referred to included F.A. Hendry and a man named Blount. Besides mapping a proper route for a canal, the three were scheduled to meet with a Captain Allen and his crew who were supposed to be sailing southward down the Kissimmee River to Lake Okeechobee. The party particularly wanted Jake along because he "had been through most of it eighteen years ago April last."[4] This, of course, was during the Civil War when Summerlin had rendezvoused with the Seminole chief, Arpeika, to discuss the lack of supplies for Arpeika's small band. He had also scouted this area along the Caloosahatchee to locate cattle for the Confederate Army and to find fords for herds of cattle that strayed to the south side of the river. And more recently, of course, he and Sam had brought cattle into the Palmdale-Fisheating Creek area.

The small survey party, which also included two men whom Jake referred to as Frasure and Hough, took a small boat near Fort Thompson. Jake wrote, "We went up the longest and deepest run I knew that we could find." Blount left the main group and followed in a small scow. As the party moved eastward toward Lake Okeechobee, tall, tough, dense patches of saw grass hindered their progress. It was the same grass that General Taylor's Indiana Volunteers found so difficult to cope with during the Battle of Lake Okeechobee in 1837. Summerlin wrote, "When we got to the end of the saw grass and west of the Ichepochee, a lake southwest of Okeechobee, we hoisted a flag some 15 or 20 feet high...designing next day to go into the lake (Okeechobee) and raise one on the edge of the lake where it could be displayed to the best advantage."[5]

The next day Blount caught up with the rest of the party and they labored on with great pain, stubbornly pushing on through the tall sharp grass with their skiff. They finally reached Lake Okeechobee — three miles from where they had placed the first flag.

Bone-tired and soaking wet, Summerlin and the rest of the party spent the night in the small boat under attack by hoards of mosquitoes. Jake wrote, "We were all wet up to our arm-pits, but we had undertaken the enterprise; and with a will and an enterprise combined, men seldom fail to accomplish their purpose." It was a paraphrase from David Livingston's book, but a passage he certainly must have believed as his determined and purposeful life had so well demonstrated.

---

[3]*Ibid.*, pp. 273-283; Karl Krismer, *Story of Fort Myers*. (Island Press, 1949), p. 31.

[4]Tebeau, *A History of Florida*, p. 280.

[5]Jacob Summerlin, notes written by Summerlin on survey of prospective canal to open waterway from Lake Okeechobee to Caloosahatchee River, 1880. (Copy of notes held by author); "From the Gulf to Lake Okeechobee," *Sunland Tribune*, 17 June 1880.

After nine days, unfortunately, Jake and his party were unable to make contact with Captain Allen's steamer, and the party returned to Fort Myers and Punta Rassa. Jake said he returned to Punta Rassa so he could begin "shipping beef to Cuba when the market opens."[6]

The development of the Kissimmee River Valley and the connection of the Caloosahatchee to Lake Okeechobee remained important to Summerlin throughout his life. When he returned to Punta Rassa, he purchased another steamer called the *Spitfire,* under the command of Captain Nelson. Once the waterway was opened, he planned to have Nelson sail the ship across the Caloosahatchee into Lake Okeechobee and up the Kissimmee River.

Summerlin saw great potential for economic development in the Kissimmee River Valley, and he wrote in 1881, "the Kissimmee has the best lands in the state, if drained, being a valley some fifteen or twenty feet below the prairies on either side and some eighty miles long, and from five to thirty-five or forty miles in width."[7] Summerlin's guess was about right, and when the Kissimmee River was straightened and deepened between 1881 and 1885 as part of the Disston Project, thousands of acres of rich land opened up as new cattle ranges and farmland. Disston's plan also made new settlements, such as Saint Cloud, Runnymeade and Ashton, possible. Kissimmee grew from a small cow camp into a town, and Central Florida prospered generally. Disston's venture, however, eventually created an ecological nightmare for the region, but there were few, if any, political or financial leaders at the time who saw such reclamation of wetlands as anything other than progress.

The Caloosahatchee was dredged "to Fort Thompson where they blasted and dug out the falls there that held back a ten foot head of water in Lake Flirt [and] the Channel tapped lake Okeechobee at More Haven. As the dredge was lifting the last earth from Lake Hickochee, there was a great deal of excitement by people in Fort Myers and other frontier settlements. A large gush of water was expected when the earth was broken loose. Summerlin sent Captain Nelson and the *Spitfire* up the Caloosahatchee filled with the curious who wanted to see this great event. A large crowd, waiting in anticipation, was disappointed when only a small trickle of water oozed out into the river.[8] A navigable canal from Lake Hickochee to Lake Okeechobee was finally opened in 1883, but the waterway was far from being practical. In September 1883, Hamilton Disston boarded the *Bertha Lee* at Fort Myers, expecting to complete the trip up the Caloosahatchee into Lake Okeechobee and through the Kissimmee River to Kissimmee in three days. It took forty-three days.[9]

---

[6]*Ibid.*

[7]*Sunland Tribune,* 17 June 1880.

[8]*Ibid.*; Marjory Stoneman Douglas, *The Everglades, River of Grass.* (New York: Rhinehart and Co., 1947), pp. 103-109; Tebeau, *A History of Florida,* p. 280.

[9]*Ibid.,* p. 107.

In order to make the route useful for boat traffic, Lake Okeechobee had to be lowered below its natural stage, a task achieved in part by canals to the Atlantic Ocean. What Summerlin, Hendry and others helped initiate was a range of new industries along the rivers from Lake Okeechobee to Fort Myers. A shipyard and factory were soon established at Kissimmee. In 1884, the *Sadie Salem* out of Boston "chugged down the coast around the tip of Florida, up past ancient Punta Rassa...through the Caloosahatchee River, Lake Okeechobee, the Kissimmee River and Lake and at last tied up at the New Kissimmee City." The famous Captain Clay Johnson was on board, the best known and most skillful pilot of Florida's inland waterways. About 1886, he bought the *Mamie Lown* at Kissimmee, a tiny oil burner, and "from that time on, Captain Johnson really was the admiral of the fleet which sailed the waterways from Okeechobee City to Kissimmee and further."

One of the first ships in his fleet was the *Mary Bell*, captained by Archie Bass. Then came the *Floridelphia*, built in Kissimmee in 1885 and named to honor Hamilton Disston, who was from Philadelphia and who had made all the new waterways possible. Other ships were soon built at Kissimmee for the new river traffic. The *Arbuckle*, the *Spray*, the *Osceola*, the *Mamie Lown*, the *Bassenger*, and the three *Naomis*, owned by Captain Ben Hall, moved cargo back and forth from Kissimmee, Okeechobee and to Fort Myers. There were twenty-one landings from Kissimmee to Fort Basinger and "many thriving little settlements." Typical of the cargo shipped out of Kissimmee for the settlers of South Florida were rolls of barbed wire, sacks of grain, bails of mail, order goods and general supplies. On their return to Kissimmee, the ships would often be loaded with boxes of fruit, naval stores, hides, furs and even raw wool. But not all the transported goods were commercial in nature. Some of the boats carried sportsmen, tourists and local residents who enjoyed the sights along the route. One excursion boat was a yacht owned by Disston, with a steel hull built at the Kissimmee yards, which once carried President Chester A. Arthur down the river on an inspection trip." But the best known excursion craft was the *Lillie*, captained by Ben Hall, which carried passengers from Kissimmee to Fort Myers for several years. The *Lillie*'s engines were cast at the Kissimmee yards. The largest excursion ship to sail from Fort Myers to Kissimmee was the *Bertha Lee*, sister ship of the *Robert E. Lee* of the Mississippi River Lee Lines. A sternwheeler, the *Bertha Lee* was 150-feet long with two smoke stacks and "thirty luxurious state rooms." However, the *Bertha Lee* proved to be too big to navigate the tight turns on the rivers and she eventually ended up on the Chattahoochee River in northwest Florida.[10]

Florida's inland river traffic had a romance of its own and, for many years, some old timers were bothered over its demise, but the revolution in railroad transportation and, eventually, automobiles made it unprofitable and impractical. The sternwheelers and sidewheelers were replaced with speed boats filled

[10]Wayne Miller, "Shifting Scenes in Florida," *The Gazette*, 1943.

with sports fishermen or other recreational boaters.

While still living in Punta Rassa, Jake and several other cattlemen were poisoned. The poisoning was described in an article in the *Tampa Tribune* in July 1881:

> Some dozen persons, including several of the most prominent cattlemen of the Caloosahatchee region, who took a meal at Col. Summerlin's house, were all attacked with severe vomiting and other symptoms of poisoning directly afterwards, and were bad sick for several days, the Colonel himself being probably the worst sufferer.
>
> There seems to have been a similar attempt at poisoning about a week before this. Colonel Summerlin ...is hardly yet fully recovered from the effects of the two doses of poison.
>
> The attending physician thinks that the poison used was either arsenic or corrosive sublimate.
>
> There are suspicions as to who was the poisoner, but so far no positive proof.[11]

On August 4, 1881, the *Bartow Informant* declared that a man named Collier had tried to poison Summerlin, Whidden and Hendry at Punta Rassa in order to get their money, but he had put too much poison in the coffee and caused them to vomit up their breakfast. However, Collier was never formally charged with the crime.[12]

Jake was bedridden for over twenty days as a result of the poisoning and the side effects continued for several years. Two years later, in 1885, he, along with his wife and a daughter, traveled to Hot Springs, Arkansas, in hopes the reputed curative powers of the warm springs would help his condition. Although Summerlin lived for another ten years, it is doubtful that he ever fully recovered from the poisoning.[13]

He offered "$500.00 for the conviction of the party who attempted to poison himself and others." The following letter from Jake appeared in the *Key West Democrat*:

> There is some person who has been stopping at this place...who is too mean for anything, and I take the privilege of stating to the public that none of us is safe from such low, mean, undermining bound wretches, for on or about the 25th of June, some one, intent upon wholesale slaughter, put corrosive sublimate in a can of parched coffee, and all of us who drank of it were made deadly sick...I cannot see any reason for the deed except the party

---

[11]Akerman, "Jacob Summerlin," *Florida Pathfinders*, p. 125; Tampa *Tribune*, 18 July 1881; Bartow *Informant*, 27 Oct. 1881, p. 1; 4 August 1881.

[12]*Ibid.*

[13]*Ibid.*, 9 June 1883, p. 3; Akerman, "Jacob Summerlin," *Florida Pathfinders*, p. 125; Bartow *Informant*, 21 July 1881.

hoped to get my safe key during the excitement and rob me. During my absence to Jacksonville, a short time before, the house was robbed and my day book was missing; no doubt the same party did this last deed.[14]

It is hard to imagine that anyone would hate Jake enough to try to kill him, but on the American frontier such mayhem and havoc were never uncommon, and anyone with the wealth and influence of people like Summerlin and Hendry might easily become targets for assassination and robbery.

By 1883, the Cuban cattle market dried up. In Key West, however, the market for cattle shipped out of Punta Rassa was strong and other local markets had also grown with Florida's population growth. By 1881, railroads became the key to most commercial expansion and Florida had 1,313 miles of railroad in operation with another 224 miles that was ready for crossties and rails. Many new lines in Florida hooked up to interstate lines. Henry Plant consolidated sixteen small railroads and secured control of South Florida. William D. Chipley, John Shelton Williams and Henry Flagler were also important figures in Florida's railroad boom during the last part of the nineteenth century. Although cattle markets were, and still are, very erratic, the new rail lines opened up new markets in the North, which offset the uncertain nature of traditional markets.[15]

Even though the prospects for the cattle industry looked promising in 1883, Jake decided to sell his Punta Rassa operation and most of his cattle and land south of Orange and Polk Counties. His sons, Sam, Jasper, George and Gideon paid him $100,000 for the operation,[16] a small fortune in 1883. If the sale had not been to members of his immediate family, he probably would have asked for more cash. He continued to own other property, including orange groves, in Orange and Polk County. Much of his wealth had been made buying and selling cattle during the flush days of the West Indian trade, and he also maintained a sizeable herd of cattle.

Jake's reasons for selling out in Southwest Florida might have been because of his declining health after the poisoning or, perhaps, his long absences from Fannie might have been the deciding factor. He moved back to Orlando in 1883, but soon grew lonesome for the cattle business. In 1888, he and a friend, Berian Platt of Plant City, purchased some real estate parcels and a one-half interest in a large herd of cattle, which grazed over sixty miles of open range all the way from Canoe Creek to Fort Bassinger.[17]

---

[14]*Ibid.*, 25 Aug. 1881 and 18 Aug. 1881.

[15]Tebeau, *A History of* Florida, pp. 269-271, 278; Brown, *Florida's Peace River Frontier*, p. 276; Akerman, *Florida Cowman*, 141.

[16]Bronson Papers.

[17]*Ibid.*

Chapter 10

The Summerlin Institute

He promoted the establishment of schools which... will doubtless be of great advantage to the country. He compared the different sects of Christians to persons passing down different streets to different churches – all would arrive at the same point at last.

Rev. S.A.W. Jewett, *Livingston in Africa*

Of all the acts of altruism for which Jacob Summerlin was given credit, perhaps none was more important than the creation and development of the Summerlin Institute at Bartow, Florida. As Charlton W. Tebeau pointed out in *A History of Florida*, "the day of tax supported education lay at least a generation in the future." The Summerlin Institute was not just another rustic private school. When it was eventually completed, its facilities, its staff, its curriculum and its mission were probably as good as any in the South for the "grades" it provided at the time.

Although Jake had no formal education, he certainly appreciated its value. Summerlin had moved to Liberty County, Georgia, so that his children could attend a recognized academy, and he also had underwritten the costs of sending the children of his brother, John Alexander, to school. John had died prematurely and his widow was left with nine children, who benefited from Jake's help.[1]

William Lloyd Harris, of Bartow, said of him, "Education was placed in the forefront of our community through the munificence of Jacob Summerlin." Jake donated forty acres for Bartow's first school in 1867. He also gave $1,120 for the construction of the first building. The Bartow Masonic Lodge, of which Jake was a member, helped in the construction of a two-story building. One floor was used for Lodge meetings and the other was used as a school. It was known

---

[1]Miller Papers; Copy of letter from Jake Summerlin to a widow, probably John Summerlin's widow, dated April 5, 1870.

as Summerlin Institute.[2]
The first Summerlin Institute opened on July 13, 1868 and the following notice was placed in the *Florida Peninsular*:

THE SUMMERLIN INSTITUTE

The Fall Term of the Institute at Bartow, South Florida, under the supervision of Adam Hill, Principal, and Stephen Sparkman, assistant, will commence on July 13, 1868. From the healthy location of the village, and the liberal patronage heretofore bestowed, the Principal flatters himself that the coming session will be largely attended.

Terms of tuition for five months for Spelling, Reading and Writing, Arithmetic, Geography, English Grammar, Composition, Philosophy, Chemistry and Botany will be $10.00. A separate schedule in Zoology and Geography will be $2.00. No deduction made except for sickness or pupil. Board for pupils may be obtained in and around the village on as good terms as the times will admit.[3]

There is no information regarding the number of students who first enrolled, but by 1873 the school had eighty-three students, which made it one of the largest schools on the frontier. The normal term was sixty-six days and the county paid two dollars per student while the patrons and parents paid six dollars per student. Jake, of course, was one of the patrons. When the school opened, W.B. Varn was superintendent of public instruction and the staff included B.F. Blount, Miss S.J. Hayman and one of Jake's sisters, Rebecca. The superintendent's salary was eighty-three dollars per term while the teachers normally received thirty dollars per term.[4]

"In the beginning of the 1880s additions and surveys added to Bartow, and it soon became necessary for the Summerlin Institute Board of Trustees, made up of Jake Summerlin, Captain D. Hughes and Colonel G.A. Hanson, to make a general sale of school lands [40 acres] at public auction and to raise a fund at once to begin the erection of a handsome school building." Initially the school

[2]B.F. Blount, "The First Summerlin Institute Is Built," Copy of letter by B.F. Blount held by author. Akerman, "Jacob Summerlin," *Florida Pathfinders*, pp. 119-120; "A Short History of International Baccalaureate School at Bartow High School," *For Virtual Visitors to the International Baccalaureate School*, pp. 1-5; Alma Hetherington, "Jake Summerlin, Pioneer Cattleman, Was 'King' of Crackers in Florida," *The Florida Times Union*, 27 June 1954; "Copy of Abstract of Deed," Sale of Fort Blount Place (170 acres) Jacob Summerlin to W.T. Carpenter, 3 March 1868.

[3]"The Summerlin Institute," *Florida Peninsular*, 13 June 1868; "Early Data on the Building of First Summerlin Institute," Old Masonic Minute Book #1 (12 June 1865-27 December 1870).

[4]"Summerlin Institute," *The Polk County Record*, 18 Nov. 1921; "Corner Stone: Grand Lodge of Masons of Florida," Bartow *Advance Courier*, 18 May 1887.

board of the Summerlin Institute had been unable to come up with enough money for the contract price of $17,000. The sale of the lands donated by Summerlin brought $8,401 and the citizens of Bartow and the surrounding area contributed another $5,000. Together this raised enough cash to begin construction and the cornerstone of the Summerlin Institute "was laid with imposing Masonic ceremonies on May 12, 1887."[5]

Summerlin was to be the featured attraction in this great affair, but since he was never one to place much stock in ceremony, he almost didn't show up for the placing of the cornerstone. Thousands of people were invited and over 300 visitors came by train. Jake chose to travel by horseback following roads and trails he had ridden over many times on cattle drives. He left a day early and spent the first night in a small hotel in Kissimmee—Florida's major cow town. It was reported that when he strode into the lobby with his saddlebags still on his shoulder, he wore no coat. His only deference to the importance of the upcoming dedication was that he brought along a pair of shoes to exchange the range boots that he normally wore. A friend of his at the hotel loaned him a nice black coat and insisted that he wear it.[6] Photographs taken at the event, however, showed that he wore no tie.

He must have been surprised by all the fanfare when he rode into Bartow. The pride of Orlando, the Coronet Band, provided a medley of marching tunes to entertain the estimated 2,500 people in attendance. Hundreds of people milled around the South Florida Depot where venison, veal, pork, beef and kid were served along with all kinds of bread, cakes, custards, pies and puddings. One reporter remarked that it was the most important event that had ever taken place in Bartow. Certainly it was an impressive gathering for the Florida frontier.

The most prominent features of the dedication were the speeches, which acknowledged the community's indebtedness to Jake for making the school possible. The most grandiose oratory came from the Master Lacy Boyd of the Masons:

Michael Angelo[sic], with his genuine and cunning chisel, liberated from the crude and shapeless marble, a beautiful angel, whose inanimate form, by the wearing of time, will pass away. You by the promptyings [sic] of your generous heart, and magnificent gift of your outstretched and charitable hand, will, for generations to come, liberate from the bonds of ignorance, and send forth thousands of polished minds and elevated hearts for noble work in life, that would have otherwise remained crude and undeveloped.[7]

---

[5]*Ibid.*
[6]Hetherington, Alma, "King of Crackers," p. 2.
[7]"Corner Stone," p. 5.

After several more speeches and presentations, Summerlin was given "a handsome, beautifully chased gold headed cane, after which the crowd responded with repeated calls of 'Uncle Jake.'"
Summerlin responded with a short speech to the crowd:

> What a generous gift! It makes me glad to receive such a gift from such a source, and I feel prouder than if I had received a kingdom...Looking in your innocent faces, where this noble work is about to be accomplished...This institute, for raising and guiding you on for good and great purposes will be honored by such pupils; continue to grow good, wise and happy, and you will have friends and parents that will be proud of such noble children.[8]

Work on the handsome brick school building was completed almost exactly one year later. The *Bartow Advance Courier* acknowledged the completion with a commemorative edition on March 7, 1888, with an article on its front page that began, "At last, through the generosity of one of nature's noblemen, Jacob Summerlin, 'King of the Crackers,' Bartow has one of the finest educational buildings in the state."[9]

In 1889, the new Summerlin Institute matriculated the first students, grades one through eleven. Later in the 1890s, a twelfth grade was added. "It was an exceptionally modern school for its days, teaching such subjects as electrodynamics, surveying...and astronomy. It was known for its advanced curriculum, liberal discipline policy and high standards of scholarship." For many years, it served as Bartow's major high school and, unfortunately, the original building was torn down in 1930. "All that remains of the original structure is a bell, embedded in cement atop a brick pillar on the grounds of the original site." Another school occupies the site, but it is not called the Summerlin Institute.

In 1897, four years after Jake's death, Colonel Joe Tillman of Quitman, Georgia, wrote one of the best descriptions of Summerlin and the Summerlin Institute that appeared in different newspapers. In an attempt to point out the advantages of a sound educational system the following appeared in the Quitman *Free Press*:

> Take for example Bartow, Florida, which twelve years ago would be termed...a straggling village of a few hundred inhabitants...This writer was present when old man Jake Summerlin...made a donation to what is known as the Summerlin Institute of $8,000...Today, owing to this donation, Bartow has a population of several thousand and the regular attendance at Summer-

---

[8]*Ibid.*, p. 7.
[9]Bartow *Advance Courier*, 7 March 1888, p. 1.

lin Institute for several years has not been less than 300 to 400. Nor is this all...Bartow has assumed proportions of a well regulated city, with block after block of elegant buildings – and the smoothest and best paved streets to be found south of Washington today.[10]

Although this was a rather extravagant appraisal of the significance of Summerlin's contributions and the importance of the Summerlin Institute, certainly Jake was a principal person in the creation and growth of Bartow and Polk County. And he certainly deserved to be called, "The father of Bartow." In an article that appeared later in the *New York Times*, December 14, 1930, Wallace Stevens wrote this tribute to Jake:

One of the famous cattle kings of this period was Jacob Summerlin, a cowboy philanthropist of the early days whose generosity made him rather a patron saint of the South Florida Range, and who left eternal monuments to his credit in Bartow and Orlando.

That he deeply missed his lack of an opportunity for a higher education was shown when he purchased a large tract of land near the heart of Bartow, county seat of Polk County, and deeded it to trustees to sell in city lots and "form a free school for the poor white children."[11]

---

[10]Colonel Joe Tillman, "Jake Summerlin," *Free Press*, 1897.

[11]Wallace Stevens, "Cattle Kings of Florida," *New York Times*, 14 Dec. 1930; p. 11.

Jacob Summerlin and his wife Frances trailed a small herd of cattle along with the bare necessities for existence into Hillsborough County shortly after they married in 1845. This is a typical family of homestead settlers moving into Central Florida. (Florida State Photographic Archives)

Chapter 11

Summerlin's Last Years in Orlando

In 1883, Jake turned over his operations at Punta Rassa to his son, Sam, and returned to live in his home in Orlando. The small hamlet had grown from seventy-eight people in 1873 to a small city with over 1,000 people. By 1884, it was estimated that the town had more than 1,600 residents and, by 1893, the population had grown to 2,900. Orlando's rapid growth could be explained by the arrival of railroads. The first tracks to Orlando were laid by the South Florida Railroad on December 1, 1880, and joined Orlando to Sanford and thus, to the St. Johns River. Several other connecting roads were soon constructed. In 1880, two Maitland residents began a track from Lake Monroe to Charlotte Harbor on the West Coast. Joseph Bumby, a friend of Summerlin who had previous railroad experience in England, became the Orlando agent for the new line. The track was later extended to Kissimmee and then to Tampa. It was later acquired by Henry Plant and became a part of the Plant System. Also in the 1880s, three short tracks were joined at Longwood, thirteen miles from Orlando. In 1886, the Midland Railroad, which ran from Longwood to Apopka then on to Kissimmee, was completed. Central and South Central Florida had a significant network of tracks by the end of the nineteenth century. Cattle were hauled over much of the East and South by rail, but more-and-more citrus and other produce moved by train. Jake, too, grew citrus in central Florida. In 1889 he sold a small grove of eight acres for $8,000.[1]

It was said that many new residents had found their way to Orlando because of Summerlin's influence. From Jacksonville, Charleston and Punta Rassa, Summerlin touted Orlando as one of the healthiest places in the state to live.[2] However, it was his infusion of gold from the West Indian cattle sales into the local economy that provided a significant part of the economic base from which

---

[1]Brown, *Hart*, 277-278, 299; Tebeau, *A History of Florida*, pp. 283, 294-295;

[2] For more information on his instrumental role in attracting residents to Orlando, see *The Historical Architectural and Archaeological Survey of Orlando, Florida*, Florida Division of Archives, History and Record Management Report Series, 1975, number 43, p. 13.

Orlando would grow.[3]
Certainly he had played a significant role in the development and growth of Central Florida, but it is unlikely that he anticipated or even wanted such a rapid population growth. There is no record regarding his feelings about this, but his wife had voiced some strong reservations about Orlando's rapid development. Jake had become concerned about the welfare of Florida's wildlife as increased numbers of hunters created pressure on the environment. An interview with Summerlin appeared in the *Orlando Reporter* in 1889 revealed his solution for saving the endangered passenger pigeon:[4]

> Where I once saw thousands of birds, I did not see one hundred; and to go now to the roosts you will find hundreds of little half-fledged birds starving to death, the parents killed or dead. It seems almost inhuman to kill them leaving their young to starve. Cannot our Florida Legislators make a tax law for hunters as well as England? If for nothing else, let it be for humanity, for if a man is able to hunt, he must be able to work.[5]

Although Summerlin sold his hotel to Nat Poyntz for $20,000, it remained a popular resort for many people visiting Orlando. Never as large or pretentious as the retreats built by Henry Flagler and Henry Plant, one reporter earlier referred to it as the "Waldorf Astoria of the day." It would change ownership several times. After Poyntz, a Mr. Harrington purchased it. The hotel was subsequently owned by Mrs. C.V. Caldwell, Neil E. Newman and J.A. Jackson, but it would always be known as the Summerlin Hotel. It was demolished in 1941 by the Sanford Wrecking Company and so ended an era in Orlando's history.[6]

Jacob Summerlin's life had born witness to some of Florida's most chaotic times. Born during Florida's turbulent Territorial days, he played a role in every major event that shaped the state for the next sixty years. From the Second Seminole War to the Civil War, he served as a volunteer soldier and enlisted on six separate occasions. He never seemed drawn to war as an exciting adventure nor saw it as a potential avenue for achieving political success.

---

[3]Brunson, "The King of the Crackers," pp. 12-17; W.R. O'Neal, "Memoirs of a Pioneer," Bronson Papers, no date nor name of newspaper, probably Orlando *Sentinel Star*.

[4] The passenger pigeon was a beautiful bird, considerably larger than the mourning dove, but very tasty, and favored by hunters. Since there were no laws regulating limits, thousands were killed, often at night. In 1813, James J. Audubon watched a flock that passed in a stream that lasted for three days. By the late 1800s, most had disappeared. The last passenger pigeon died in a Cincinnati zoo in 1914. "Passenger Pigeon," *The World Book*, Vol. P, 1965.

[5]"License for Hunters," *Florida Times Union*, 13 April 1889.

[6]Frisbie, "An Era in Orlando," *The Polk County Democrat*, p. 13; John Forney Rudy, "Romance That Is Orlando Built Around Summerlin Hotel, Now Being Wrecked," Orlando *Sentinel Star*, 1941.

To him military service was a duty. Consequently, he never sought promotion or command and he usually served as a private or a scout.

Florida became a state in 1845, the same year that Jake married Frances Knight Zipperer, a woman of remarkable qualities who was as dedicated to frontier life and hard work as he was. Married for forty-eight years, Jake and Frances raised seven children, all of whom led successful lives and several of whom became successful cattlemen. A builder of towns, a planner, a surveyor and a promoter of new transportation routes, he helped to establish new markets for one of Florida's most plentiful and valuable resources, the cracker cow.

Summerlin possessed skills and strengths that allowed him to survive and prosper on the frontier, but what distinguished him for many of his peers was his empathy with and compassion for those people poorer than he was, his concern for the needs of his community and his willingness to share his wealth to help with both. His honesty and experience served him well in helping to bring peace to Central Florida's range wars and in dealing with the Native Americans.

On November 1, 1893, Jake Summerlin died at his home in Orlando. According to his son, Sam, who administered his estate, there was some question about the "circumstances" surrounding his death. What these circumstances were was never recorded, and the real cause or causes remain a mystery. However, several sources reported that he suffered from "dropsy," a common diagnosis for the time. Perhaps, the poisoning he experienced when he lived at Punta Rassa affected his general health.[7]

His funeral and burial took place in Bartow, Florida. The *Democratic Leader* carried the following details regarding the services:

A vast concourse of people, led by the Masonic Lodge with P.M.J.W. Boyd as acting master, assembled to do him honor, while the beautiful and impressive service of the Episcopal Church was read by Rev. J.H. Davet of St. James Church, Tallwood, Florida.

The Reverend Davet was assisted by Reverend Shipp of the Methodist Episcopal Church of Bartow, Reverend Nash of the Baptist Church and Reverend E.C. McKinley of the Presbyterian Church. Summerlin was buried at Oak Hill Cemetery in Bartow.

His death was reported in newspapers all over the state. Obituaries also appeared in some Georgia newspapers. The Bartow *Democrat and Leader* lamented, "Like some giant of old, before whom men instinctively bow, was his life and name to the people of Bartow"[8] His beloved wife, Fannie, died four

---

[7]Akerman, "Jacob Summerlin," *Florida Pathfinders*, pp. 125-126.

[8]Frisbie, "End of the Road," *The Polk County Democrat*, 3 December 1973, p. 23.

years later and was buried next to him at Oak Hill.

One reporter accused Jake of "ostentatious humility" and perhaps there was some truth to this. However, his humility seemed genuine, and he surely would have felt uncomfortable with the many accolades that were paid to him. After all, he declared, "I am nothing under the sun but a native-born sun baked old Florida Cracker."

Epilogue

Although considered to be Florida's wealthiest and most successful cattleman for over two decades, Jake Summerlin died with debts attached to his estate. Leaving no will, his estate was administered by his youngest, and perhaps his closest, son, Samuel. Samuel estimated that his entire estate was only worth $1,100, which included 180 head of cattle that ranged in Orange and Osceola Counties. This was a far cry from the days when he estimated his herds at 20,000 head. Other items in the estate included two horses, two wagons, some unspecified farm fixtures and a negligible amount of house furniture. Neither real estate parcels nor buildings were listed. An obituary in a Ft. Myers newspaper indicated that when he died he was one of the richest men in Florida with an estimated fortune of $40,000 to $50,000.

Creditors to the estate included J.J. Patrick, J. Percy Keating, M.R. Marks and Carl Marks, all of Orlando. His debts were over $5,000. His son, Jasper, who had accrued a sizeable cattle herd and other properties, helped to pay off a part of these debts and presumably other members of the family chipped in to clear all debts by 1896.

It is unclear as to what happened to Jake's large real estate holdings, his cattle and other assets. As late as 1880, he had received $100,000 for his cattle operation, and in 1888, the year the Summerlin Institute opened in Bartow, he purchased one-half interest in a large cattle and real estate adventure along with Berrian Platt of Plant City.

During Reconstruction, he invested in some of Florida's prime property. One piece of property in present day Tampa, known as Hooker's Point, was located to the east of the military reserve and surrounded by water. Summerlin's close friend, Governor Ossian Hart, had always recognized Tampa's waterways as having great potential for economic growth and had strongly supported its development. Summerlin also had owned sizeable tracts of land in Orange, Polk, Manatee and Monroe Counties.

While the value of Florida real estate has long been a major component in its economic system, it was not so potentially profitable during Summerlin's time as it is today. Neither cattlemen nor entrepreneurs could generally expect land investments alone to cover unwise or unfortunate investments during bad times. Few cattlemen during the nineteenth century purchased large sections of land in the days of open range. Kyle VanLandingham, a historian of Florida's pioneer families, explains that it was not at all unusual for a well-to-do stockman to suddenly become insolvent over a short time. Some modern day cattlemen claim that things haven't changed all that much. Nineteenth Century cattle barons, such as Abner Johnston, John Collier, J. W. Whidden and Captain William Hooker, had periods of financial difficulty. Even the generally lucrative West Indian trade was capricious and fluctuated with the outbreaks of civil unrest that plagued Cuba between 1868 and 1898. Of course, domestic depressions, such as those in 1873 and 1893, had impacts on cattle sales. Sometimes these crashes occurred so rapidly that boom times became gloom times overnight.

A letter, penned by Summerlin on April 5, 1870, demonstrated that he was not always rich. Writing to a woman, probably a widowed sister-in-law, he apologized for not being in a position at the time to help her or her children, presumably with educational expenses. Summerlin wrote, "I have been anxious to do something for you for sometime but I have had some of the worst luck I could have had. I lost nearly all the stock I own." The reason for his loss was not clear, but he wrote that he had been losing as many as 180 head of cattle a month. Always sympathetic toward widows, Summerlin offered to take in two or three of her children and to send them to school. A few years later he seemed to have recouped his losses, at least in part, since he was taxed for 2,500 head of cattle in Manatee County and for $13,005 in personal property in Orange County. His son, Jasper, who acted as an agent for him in Polk County, was taxed for 360 acres at about the same time. The transfer of property to his children before his death could explain his insolvency at the end of his life.

Besides his financial holdings over the years, his works of community charity and his concern and compassion for the poor distinguished Jake's life. An openhanded use of his resources, even during his own hard times, marked his commitment to these causes.

His legendary status, particularly within the cattle industry, continues today in Florida.

Appendix A

Chronology

1783-1785: Joseph Summerlin, probably grandfather of Jacob Summerlin, Junior, served in Tonyn's Rangers.

1793-1848: Jacob Summerlin, Senior (Summerell).

1812-1814: Jacob Summerlin, Senior, became U.S. citizen after fighting in War of 1812. Signed petition for East Florida Republic to become part of the U.S.

1813: Jacob Summerlin, Senior, part of survey party for laying out settlement in district of Elotchoway [*sic*].

Jacob Summerlin, Senior, lived at Fernandina and knew John Q. Adams and Lors de Onis while they were negotiating Adams-Onis Treaty. Florida Purchase Treaty.

1819: Jacob, Senior, moved from Mandarin to Alligator and traded with Indians on both sides of St. Mary's River. He established a farm in present day Columbia County and married Lydia Lang of Camden County, Georgia, who dies a year later.

1821: Mary Ann Hagan, a widow, married the Jacob Summerlin, Senior.

1820: Jacob Summerlin, Junior, was born at Alligator (Lake City). According to family legend, he was born in a nearby fort during Indian attack. The same legend also claimed he was the first white child born in Territory of Florida.

1828: Mary Hagan Summerlin, who was very ill, left Lake City for Jefferson County to be with her mother, Nancy Cone Hagan.

1830: Florida Census, Tax rolls. First Federal census involving Florida.

1832: Alligator became county seat of Columbia County.

1835-1842: Jacob, Senior, Jacob, Junior, and John Summerlin served in various militia units against Seminoles. Jacob, Senior, organized his own company.

1835-1842: During the Second Seminole War. John, Jacob, Senior, and Jacob, Junior, played active roles in hostilities.

1836: Mary Hagan Summerlin, wife of Jacob Summerlin, Senior, died.

1841: Samuel Knight, Jake's father-in-law, made a journey to Hillsborough County to find open ranges for cattle. There were few settlers in this area at time.

1842: Armed Occupation Act passed by Congress (a Homestead Act).

1843: Jacob Summerlin, Senior, elected to Territorial Legislative Council. He served in Senate and House and was appointed to important committees. He was registered as a Whig and was opposed to Florida Territory becoming a state. John Summerlin acted as Senator messenger.

1844: After marrying Frances Knight Zipperer, a widow, Jake drove a herd of cattle to Knight's Station and homesteaded near Samuel Knight, his father-in-law. Summerlin served as the first postmaster of Hickpocksassa and as a deputy sheriff.

Jacob Summerlin

1845: Legislative Act legally changes Jacob Summerall to Summerlin. Florida became a state (a month before Texas did).

1848: Died: Jacob Summerlin, Senior. Jacob Summerlin, Junior allegedly inherited slaves in a will probated at Alligator.

1851: Jake led a search party for a kidnapped white boy. A period of Indian-settler hostility began 1848.

1858: Summerlin sold his store and cotton gin in order to devote himself full time to the cattle business.

1859: Summerlin, in business with James McKay, shipped first cattle to Havana that summer. By December, over 2,400 beeves had been shipped and Summerlin furnished many of them.

1860: Tax roles for Hillsborough County valued Summerlin's personal property at $90,000. He owned over 2,100 head of cattle in Hillsborough County, along with shipping pens at Manatee River, Tampa, Peace River and Cedar Key.

1861: Summerlin moved his family to Ft. Ogden on Peas Creek and acquired 10,000 head of beef when he acquired the Hooker herd with the help of McKay. He received a two-year contract from the Confederate Government to furnish 25,000 head of beef to the army at the rate of 600 head per week. His own herd produced an estimated 5,000 to 8,000 head annually. Summerlin was commissioned a sergeant in CSA. He bought Ft. Blount in 1862.

1863-1864: Summerlin furnished McKay with beeves for cargo for blockade runners. Summerlin went to Cuba.

1865: Jake participated in largest attack by Cow Cavalry when Cow Calvary attacked Fort Myers where a large number of Union troops were stationed. Summerlin was a scout on this raid.

1865-1866: The Summerlin family lived at Fort Meade.

1865-1866: The Summerlin family lived in Bartow (Fort Blount), where Jake donated land to churches and for the creation of a school.

1867: Jake moved his family to Liberty County, Georgia, so his children could be educated at Walthourville Academy.

1869: Summerlin established a new cattle market in Savannah. He also sold 1,500 cattle to Spanish officials in Cuba and shipped them from Ft. Ogden.

1871: Summerlin was appointed to clear out Peas Creek.

1873: Summerlin moved to the hamlet of Orlando, possibly because of wife's health. He and family were very involved in town activities. Summerlin was able to establish Orlando as county seat; and he donated the land around Lake Eola to the city for a park. He also built a fine hotel and bought a dry goods store although he longed for work cattle. He had 20,000 cattle at this time from Orange County southward to Caloosahatchee River.

1874: Jake moved to Punta Rassa and built a large "bunk house" for cowmen. Punta Rassa became cattlemen's harbor and haven. More than 1,000 acres of cattle pens held cattle destined for Cuba. According to one estimate, 1,600,000 cows were shipped from Punta Rassa to Cuba from 1874 to 1884.

1876: Jake and son, Sam, moved the first cattle herd into lower Fisheating Creek near Palmdale. This range became one of the best and largest in Florida.

1879: Summerlin led a survey party from the headwaters of the Caloosahatchee River to Lake Okeechobee to map a possible canal from Lake Okeechobee to the Caloosahatchee River.

1883: Jake sold his herd and some land to sons for over $100,000 and moved back to Orlando. He still bought cattle and spent time on favorite horse, *Old Morgan*.

1893: Summerlin died in Orlando. His passing was noted all over Florida and Georgia. He was buried in Bartow.

1896: Frances Summerlin, Jake's wife, died and was buried next to her husband.

Appendix B

Retyped Version of a Copy of Will Made From Original
Jacob Summerlin, Senior

State of Florida – County of Columbia – In the Name of God, Amen.

I, Jacob Summerlin, of the county and state aforesaid, being weak in body but sound of mid and disposing memory and knowing that it is once appointed to all men to die do make, ordain, constitute and appoint this my last will and testament.

1st, I assign my soul to God who gave it and my body to the dust to be buried at the discretion of my friends.

With regard to the affairs of this world with what it has pleased Almighty God to bless me with I gave and bequeath in manner and form as follows to wit: 1st I gave and bequeath to my wife, Mary Ann Elizabeth Summerlin, one negro man named Eddy, aged about 28 years, and one negro woman, named Harriett, aged about 24 years, to have and to hold the aforesaid negro slaves unto her the said Mary Ann Elizabeth Summerlin, her heirs and assignees forever.

2nd, I gave and bequeath unto my daughter, Rebecca Summerlin, one negro boy, named Toney, aged about 10 years and one negro girl, named Mahala, aged about 11 years to have and to hold the aforesaid negro slaves unto her the said Rebecca Summerlin her heirs and assigns forever.

3rd, I gave and bequeath unto my daughter, Louise Ann Summerlin, one negro boy, named Young, aged about 7 years, and one negro girl named Sarah Ann, aged 8 years, to have and to hold the aforesaid negro slaves unto her the said Louise Ann Summerlin her heirs and assigns forever.

4th, I gave and bequeath to my daughter Caroline Victoria, one negro boy, named Granville, aged about 7 years, and one negro girl, named Esther, aged about 2 years to have and to hold the aforesaid negro slaves unto the said Caroline Victoria Summerlin, her heirs and assigns forever.

5th, All the balance of my estate after payment of my just debts to be equally divided among my dutiful heirs.

6th, And it is also my desire that a certain mulatto girl named Fanny, aged about 10 years, shall not be set apart as a part of my estate to be distributed as such among my heirs but that said mulatto girl, Fanny, will live and be in charge and under the care and protection of my wife, Mary Ann Elizabeth Summerlin, until the said girl, Fanny, should have arrived at the age of 21 years, which time it is my request that she be at liberty to act for herself with my wife Mary Ann Elizabeth Summerlin as her guardian.

It is my will and desire that my son John A. Summerlin and my two sons-in-law Thomas D. Dexter and Robert Brooks should act as executors to this, my last will and testament and that a division of my estate shall take place as soon after my death as they the said executors shall deep practicable.

And it is my further will and desire that my son, John A. Summerlin and my two sons-in-law, Thomas D. Dexter and Robert Brooks should act as guardians for my two younger children.

Hereby ratifying and confirming this and no other to be my last will and testament.

Signed, sealed in presence of

This 13th day of January A.D. 1848

(Signed) Jacob Summerlin, Senior

A.A. Stewart, Justice of the Peace

A.B. Wood

N.C. Stewart

State of Florida, County of Columbia. Probate Court at Chambers, Jan. 18th, 1848.

Personally appeared before me A. A. Stewart, who being duly sworn sayest that he verily believes that this written instrument of writing to be the last will and testament of Jacob Summerlin and that he saw the said Jacob Summerlin sign and publish this same as his last will and testament and that the deposition signed the same as a subscribing witness thereon in the presence of the testator and that he also saw A. B. Wood and N. C. Stewart do so likewise.

Signed A. A. Stewart

Sworn and subscribed before me this 18th day of Jan. A.D. 1848.

Signed James S. Jones, Judge of Probate

CC

State of Florida County of Columbia, I James S. Jones, Judge of Probate do hereby certify that the forgoing is a true and correct copy of the original will on file in my office at Alligator. Given under my hand and probate seal (haveing no seal of office) this 18th day of Jan. 1848.

James S. Jones, C.

Appendix C

Hillsborough County
Itchepucksassa Oct. 2 1850
To your Excelency Governor Brown

Dr Sir I have just returned from another scout last week hoping to hear of the Child that was lost or stolen from Ms. Sumners previous and making discovery of Indian sine whitch caused us to go and See if we could not find Some more) And I thought it the duty of us to let you know how clost by we ware connected.

We started from my hous on the 23 of Sept and the first day we made no discovery but the 24 late in the Evning we saw some new burnt woods acrost a glade in the head of the Withleocoochee and trid to get to it (for we was certain we would find some sine) but we could not cross the glade and on the 25 we started Early and in about 2 miles of whare we camped after crossing a slew of mud and swamp we come out in and Indian field they had not left more than 4 days they had clered and planted it this year there was corn pees potatoes and other vegetables growing we went acrost the field (on the same Island for it was all an Island of about 50 acres) we came to there houses there was 9 houses in all or we might call them camps there was 5 built hose roof fashion coverd with Cipress bark and boards and 4 built flat roof fashion Every thing that they left that was of any value was carefully stuck up as though they intended to come back we supposed that they took a scare at the Scout that was out before there looked to be sine enough for 25 or 30 Indians at the lowest and there was but 6 of us though there was few of us we wanted to find the child but we found nothing at there camp that would lead to the discovery of the child only one shirt sleev that we brough[t] home and as soon as a chance will offer we will send it to Mr. Sumner and we expect him or his family will know it there Camp is about 25 miles North E of here and I live on the Fort Mellon road it is also in a Northern direction from Gen Twigs Camp about 40 miles they are on our ground there is no dout and you may suppose our feelings when we send a child on an errand or to school for we are persuaded to believe that the Indians have got the lost child

We are getting tired of waiting to see what government will do and we calculate to scout until we are satisfied what has become of the Child and I fear if we find the child in thare possession there will be a fight if they don't gave him up and we hope to have company enough the next time to fight our way for we

126

ware in a very dangerous place being that there was so few of us we Scouted
until the 29 and found sine occasionaly but did not come up with the Indians
   I have seen your letter in the Florida Sentinell whitch gave me some hopes but
I would find a greater relief if I was to hear that they had to go to Arkansas
      You will pleas Excuse bad Scollarship
      Nothing more but remain your Obedient Servant
               Jacob Summerlin

   [Transcribed from a copy of the original in the Florida State Archives,
Record Group 101, Series 755, Carton 2, Folder 4, Tallahassee, Florida, by Joe
Knetsch on August 13, 1997.]

Appendix D

Prince Johnson

One of Jake's best friends was a former slave named Prince Johnson. Jake bought Prince from a Mr. Turner in 1863. Below is the 1870 census from Alachua County.

Johnson, Prince	50
Judy	40
Bruno	22
Hector	8
Jack	51
Cassey	2

Prince Johnson had a brother named Jacko. His mother may have been Judy, b.c. 1790, in South Carolina.

Appendix E

Capt. F. A. Hendry's Independent Cavalry, Munnerlyn's Battalion

Soldier.. Dschg

Captain Francis A. Hendry.....................................5/20/65
1st Lieutenant T. C. M. Boggess.....................................5/20/65
2nd Lieutenant John E. Fewell 5/20/65
3rd Lieutenant George W. Hendry 5/20/65

Enlisted Men

Altman, William...5/20/65
Altman, William M ....   "
Blount, Benjamin F...   "
Blount, John C ....   "
Blount, J. J...   "
Carney, William ....   "
Carron, Joseph..   "
Chandler, S. M ....   "
Curry, Zora ....   "
Durrence, John R...   "
Flint, Martin ....   "
Flint, William R................/64.............................   "
Godwin, R.[?] A..   "
Godwin, Solomon M ....   "
Green, James................../64.............................   "
Hendry, A. J...   "
Hendry, W. M...   "
Hogan, F. B..   "
Hollingsworth, W. K ....   "
Hollingsworth, Sam C..Deserted
Jones, Thomas...   "
Keen, E. B................7/13/64.............................   "
Mitchell, George W ....   "
Parker, Streaty ....   "
Pearce, John M..   "
Pearce, P. S ....   "
Prescott, Nelson...................................Deserted to the enemy
Prine, Jackson ....   "

Rainey, Joseph...................../63.. "
Sapp, John.......................5/64.. "
Skipper, John .... "
Smith, James J....................................Transferred to Capt. John Parsons' Co.
Smith, William... "
Summerlin, Jacob... "
Summerlin, Jasper.. "
Snow, Morgan .... "
Tillis, Willoughby .... "
Varn, William .... "
Wilson, Frank J .... "
Willingham, W. H..............Accidentally wounded while on drill by comrade
who thought his gun was not loaded
Wiggins, R. C.....................6/15/64.. "
Zipperer, Gideon.. "
McClellan, J. L................./63.. "

See David W. Hartman, Compiler, David Coles, Associate Compiler, *Biographical Rosters of Florida's Confederate and Union Soldiers 1861-1865*, 6 volumes, (Wilmington, N. C. 1995), Volume V, pp. 2010-2018, for a roster of the First Florida Cow Cavalry, Company A. Of Captain Francis Asbury Hendry (1833-1917), they wrote in part: "When the Civil War broke out, he joined the Confederate Commissary Department, but left in 1863 to raise his own company of cavalry. Major Munnerlyn rated Hendry's company as the most efficient and reliable in the entire battalion. His company reversed the misfortune that the Confederates had been experiencing in southwest Florida."

The following sources deal with Munnerlyn's attack on Fort Myers: Henry A. Crane to Henry W. Bowers, April 15, 1864, Dept. and Dist. of Key West, 1861-68, R.G. 393, National Archives; P.W. White Papers, Alma Clyde Field Library of Florida History, Cocoa, FL; "Old Papers Belonging to Capt. F.A. Hendry, filed in Lee County, FL, Circuit Court by Mrs. J.F. Menge"; James McKay, Senior, to Pleasant W. White, Jan. 7, Feb. 4, March 25, 1864, Pleasant W. White Papers, Alma Clyde Field Library of Florida History, Cocoa, FL; Joe A. Akerman, *Florida Cowman, A History of Florida Cattle Raising*, Florida Cattlemen's Assoc. (Kissimmee, FL) 1976-1999, pp. 91-95; *Records of Rebellion*, Series I, Vols. 49 and 53; Series IV, Vol. 3, 47; Hanna, A.J. and Hanna, Kathryn, *Lake Okeechobee: Willspring of the Everglades*, Bobbs-Merrill (New York: 1948) p. 84; Theodore Lesley, "Confederate Cattle Battalion of Florida, Speech delivered to Florida Historical Society, " (copy in *Florida Cowman, A History of Florida Cattle Raising*, pp. 88-89); L.B. Northrop, "Communique to Confederate Secretary of War," *Records of Rebellion*, Series III, Vol. III, pp. 730-731; Charles J. Munnerlyn to William Miller, Dec. 10, 1864, Hendry Papers; Canter Brown, Junior, *Florida's Peace River Frontier*, University of Central Florida Press (Orlando:1992), pp. 166-167, 171-175; Robert A. Taylor, "Cow Cavalry: Munnerlyn's Battalion in Florida," *Florida Historical Quarterly*, Vol. 65, October, 1986, pp. 196-214; David M. Bamford and Kyle S. VanLandingham, "Now Just Hold Your Cow Cavalry Horses!" http://www.geocities.com/yes_album/rebuttal.html; Frances C. Morgan Boggess, *A Veteran of Four Wars: The Autobiography of F.C.M. Boggess* (Arcadia, FL, 1900)69; Report of Capt. James Doyle, 110 New York Infantry, (Fort Myers, Fl: 21/Feb/1865) *Official Records*, Series I – Vol. XLIX/I [S#103].

Bibliography

Official Records, Manuscripts and Letters

"Abstract of Corrective Deed. Jacob and Francis Summerlin, G.A. Hanson and David Hughes." Deed Book "Q." Bartow, 12 March 1886, p. 497.

"Abstract of Deed. Jacob Summerlin to W.T. Carpenter." Deed Book "B." Bartow, 18 February 1867, p. 2.

"Bounty Land Grant made out to Riley D. Blount" (Part of Frisbie Papers), Bartow.

Bronson, Anna F. Interview about Summerlins. Kissimmee: July 14, 1991.

"Bronson Papers." Includes newspaper articles, letters, poems, pictures about Summerlins, Bronsons, Barbers, Fertics, etc., owned by Mrs. Anna F. Bronson of Kissimmee.

Brown, Thomas Governor. "Correspondence Between 1849-1853." Box 2, Folder 4, Series 755, R.G.101. Tallahassee: Florida State Archives.

"Carpenter, D.A. Pension Agent." Letter to William Lochner, Commissioner of Pensions. Knoxville: U.S. Pension Agency. 5 September 1895.

Coleman, Helen H. "Genealogical Data on Summerlin Family," Gainesville: August 1, 1988.

"Comptroller's Vouchers of Hillsborough County, 1849. "RG 350, Series 565, Box 3. Tallahassee: Florida State Archives.

Crane, Henry A. Captain (USA) Second Regiment Florida Calvary. "Letters Regarding Jacob Summerlin." Records of U.S. Army Continental Commands, 1821-1920, Vol. I, Entry 2269. Gainesville: P.K. Yonge Library.

Cresap, Ida Keeling, "Pioneer Cattlemen, Ranges, Markets and Customs." *The History of Florida Agriculture: The Early Era.* (Unpublished manuscript), Gainesville, FL.

"Cuss Finger," Correspondence on Florida cattle industry, Fort Ogden, 1879.

Dowling, Dan J. "Sketch of Seminole War and Sketches During a Campaign by a Lieutenant of the Left Wing." Charleston: 1836.

"East Florida Papers, 1812-1813." Bundle 112H9, microcopy roll number 42, St. Augustine: St. Augustine Historical Society.

"Federal and State Census Records. Agricultural Records for 1880." R.G. 1020, Series 548. Tallahassee: Florida State Archives.

Ferrell, Tommie. "Notes, letters, newspaper articles on early cattle trade at Punta Rassa, Florida." Tallahassee.

"Florida Census, 1830." Microcopy number 19, Roll number 15. Tallahassee: Florida State Archives.

"Florida Tax Rolls by Counties, 1830-1880." Microcopies. Tallahassee: Florida State Archives.

General Headquarters of the Army. "Letterbooks." R.G. 108, Washington: National Archives.

Harris, Buchner, "Letters Regarding 'Legislative Council' of East Florida." File 2, Box 60, Loc. No. 1760 – 1812. 16 June 1813. Atlanta: Department of Archives and History.

Hauser, Sidney in *Edge of Wilderness* (adapted from Register of Postmaster), Washington: National Archives.

Hawk, Robert (ed). "Florida Militia Muster Rolls of Seminole Wars," Vols. 3, 4, 7 and 72, St. Augustine: Florida Department of Military Affairs.

Horn, Helen, "Papers on Summerlins, etc." Cave Creek, AZ, August 5, 2004.

"Internal Improvement Fund Correspondence," R.G. 593, Series 914, Box 12 (1866-1867). Tallahassee: Florida State Archives.

Johnston, Lela Summerlin, "Letter regarding William Towles," Fort Myers, FL, April 27, 1978. In possession of authors.

Lesley, Theodore. "Papers Including Diaries, Letters, Newspaper Articles, and Bill of Sales Regarding Early Florida Cattle Industry." (Location of papers now unknown). Tampa, 1976.

"Letter from Cedar Keys," Savannah *Morning News*, 15 July 1880, p.1.

McKay, James. "Correspondence During Civil War Regarding Sale and Movement of Cattle in Florida." Tampa: University of South Florida.

"Marriage Book I, Alachua County Florida." 8 February 1845. (Marriage record of Frances Zipperer and Jacob Summerlin).

Miller, Jan. "Papers on Jacob Summerlin, Junior, one copy of letter written by Summerlin in 1870." Fort Pierce, FL, 2004.

Orange County Clerk of Court, "Papers on Jacob Summerlin, Junior Estate, 1893," Orlando, 2004.

Platt, Bessie Summerlin. "Genealogical Data of Summerlin Family," (Part of Louise Frisbie Papers). Bartow: 1977.

"Service Records of Volunteer Soldiers." Microcopies, RG 1025, 608, Roll 30. Tallahassee: Florida State Archives.

Summerlin, "Fannie." "Declaration of Widow for Pension," (Indian War Pensions), Act of July 27, 1892. Washington, DC: National Archives.

Summerlin, Jacob. "Description of Jacob Summerlin, Junior Activities During Second Seminole War." Record and Pension Office, Washington, DC: War Department.

Summerlin, Jacob. "Letter From Visitor Appearing in Tampa *Guardian*," 14 August 1880, p. 2.

"Summerlin Institute, Data on Building First Summerlin Institute," *Minute Books of Bartow's First Masonic Lodge*. 12 June 1865, 27 December 1870, 6 April 1885.

Turner, Frederick Jackson, "The Significance of the Frontier in American History," copy of paper given at World's Columbian Exposition, Chicago: 1893.

"Unconfirmed Claims," *Spanish Land Grants in Florida*, Vol. I, Historical Records Survey Division of Community Service Programs, WPA. Tallahassee: Florida State Archives, 1942.

"U.S. Census of Wayne County Georgia," Microfilm 89, roll number 9, Tallahassee: Florida State Archives.

"U.S. Coast and Geodetic Survey." Section VI, General Reconnaissance of Western Coast of Florida, 1848 – 1851, Washington, DC: National Archives.

VanLandingham, Kyle. "Notes, Letters, Genealogical Records, Newspaper Articles on Florida Cattle Industry." Riverview, FL.

"Warranty Deed, Jacob Summerlin to Trustees of Methodist Church of Bartow, FL." 29 March 1884.

Articles and Books

"Bartow High Has Proud History." *The Polk County Democrat*. Bartow: 11 May 1987, pp. 4-5.

"Biographical Sketch of Jacob Summerlin, Founder of Summerlin Institute." *Bartow Advance-Courier*, 25 May 1887.

Blankner, Mary Huffaker. "Summerlin Institute," *Polk County Historical Quarterly*, Vol. 15, September, 1988, pp. 2-3.

Brown, Canter. *Ossian Bingley Hart*. Baton Rouge: Louisiana State University, 1997.

Brown, Canter. *Tampa, In Civil War and Reconstruction*. Tampa: University of Tampa Press, 2000.

Brown, Canter. "Philip and Morris Dzialynski: Jewish Contributions to the Rebuilding of the South," *American Jewish Archives*. Cincinnati: Campus of Hebrew Union College, 1992.

Brown, Canter. *Florida Peace River Frontier*. Gainesville: Florida Presses, 1988.

Burnett, Gene. "Florida's Cattle Monarch." *Florida Trend Magazine*, November, 1917.

Canova, Andrew P. *Life and Adventure in South Florida*. Palatka: 1885, pp. 71-72.

"Captain Jacob Summerlin," (St. Augustine) *The News*, 30 July 1842, p. 2.

Carter, Clarence (ed). *Territorial Papers of the United States, Florida Territory*, Vols. XXIV, XXVI, XXIII. Washington, 1956 – 1962.

Carter, Clarence (ed). *Territorial Papers of the United States, Florida Territory*. Vol. XXV, pp. 163 – 166.

Cassidy, Daniel G. "Cork." *The Illustrated History of Florida Paper Money*.

"Cattle Kings of Florida," *New York Times*, 14 December 1930, p. 11.

"Columbia Sheriff's Sale." (Jacksonville) *The News*, 3 November 1849, p. 1.

"Correspondence from New York." (Palatka) *South Eastern Herald*, 25 September 1875, p. 1.

Covington, James W. *The Story of Southwestern Florida*, Vol. I and II. New York: Lewis Historical Publishing.

Covington, James W. *The Seminoles of Florida*. Gainesville: The University Press of Florida, 1993.

"Cow Hunters." (Tampa) *The Weekly Floridian*, 24 June 1884.

Crow, Mary Hilliard. *Old Tales and Trails of Florida*. St. Petersburg: Osceola County Historical Society, 1987, pp. 15, 17, 46, 48, 51, 53, 56, 79, 94, 138 and 193.

Curtis, A.H. "Botanical Explorations in Southern Florida." *Florida Dispatch*, Vol. II, 1883.

"Dancy, Lt. to Quartermaster General," July 31, 1835.

Jacob Summerlin

Davidson, Alvie (Compiler). *Florida Land: Records of the Tallahassee and Newnansville General Land Office, 1825-1892*. Bowie, Maryland: Heritage Books, Inc., 1989.

Denham, James M., and Canter Brown, Junior, (Editors). *Cracker Times and Pioneer Lives*. Columbia: University of South Carolina, 2000.

Devane, Albert. "Jacob Summerlin, Junior," *Early Florida History*, Vol. I.

"Executor's Sale: Jacob Summerlin, Senior," St. Augustine *Herald*, 8 December 1849.

Fries, Kena. *In the Long, Long Ago, Orlando and Now*. Orlando: Florida Press, 1938.

Frisbie, Louise K. "Jacob Summerlin Left Lasting Legacy." *The Polk County Democrat*, 11 May 1987, pp. 14-15.

Frisbie, Louise K. *Peace River Pioneers*. Miami: E.A. Publishing, Inc., pp. 32-35; pp. 47-49.

Frisbie, Louise K. "Jacob Summerlin." (Bartow) *The Democrat and Leader* (A series of articles on Jacob Summerlin and his family), 2 October 1973 to 26 November 1973.

"From the Gulf to Okeechobee." *The Sunland Tribune*, 17 June 1880.

Fuller, Hubert B. *The Purchase of Florida* (Facsimile Reproduction of 1906 edition). Gainesville: University of Florida Press, 1964, pp. 374-394.

Gordon, Julius J. *Biographical Census of Hillsborough County, Florida, 1850*. Tampa: Polk County Historical Genealogical Library, 1989.

Graff, Mary. *Mandarin on the St. Johns*. Gainesville: University of Florida Press, 1963, pp. 6-7.

Gran, Sara Nell. "Captain Francis Asbury Hendry (1833-1917) Soldier, Cattle King, Statesman, Historian, Benefactor." *Florida Cattle Frontier Symposium, 1845-1895*. Kissimmee: Florida Cattlemen's Association and Florida Cracker Cattle Breeder's Association, 1995.

Hanna, Alfred Jackson and Hanna, Kathryn A. "Cow Cavalry" in *Lake Okeechobee: Wellspring of the Everglades*. American Lake Series (Reprint) Dunwoody, Georgia: Norman S. Buz (?), 1973, pp. 72-75.

Hawes, Leland. "Former Rebels Saw Error of Their Ways." *The Tampa Tribune*, 3 June 1990, p. 4-H.

Hetherington, Alma. "Jake Summerlin, Pioneer Cattleman," (Jacksonville) *Florida Times Union*, 27 June 1954.

"Jake Summerlin." *The Sunland Tribune*, 5 August 1880.

Journal of Proceedings of Legislative Council of Territory of Florida, 1843. Tallahassee: J. Knowles Printer, 1845, pp. 40-48, p. 84; p. 115.

Kennedy, Stetson. *Palmetto Country*. Reprint. Tallahassee: Florida A&M University Press, 1989.

Keuchel, Edward F. *A History of Columbia County, Florida*. Tallahassee: Sentry Press, 1981.

Knetsch, Joe. *Florida's Seminole Wars, 1817-1858*. Charleston: Arcadia Publishing, 2003.

"Land Claims Near Dade City." *Southern Journal*, 9 June 1846, p. 176.

'Latchua Country News. "Territorial Papers of the United States," *Latchua Country News*, Vol. 2, Gainesville: 15 January 1987, pp. 7-9.

Livingston, Richard. *South Florida Pioneers*. Fort Myers: January, 1980, pp. 25-35; July, 1978, pp. 17-18.

McKay, D.B. "Story of Mrs. Blount Recalls Rugged Days." *Tampa Sunday Tribune*, 26 September 1948.

McKay, D.B. (ed.). *Pioneer Florida*, Vols. I and II. Tampa: Southern Publishing Co., 1959.

McNeely, Ed. *A History of Polk County Florida*. Bartow: Polk County Historical Commission.

Mahon, John K. *History of the Second Seminole War, 1835-1842*. Gainesville: University of Florida Press, 1985, p. 179.

Matthews, Janet Snyder. *Edge of Wilderness*. Tulsa: Caprine Press, 1983.

Mealor, Theodore, Junior and Merle Prunty. "Open Range Ranching in Southern Florida." Reprint from *Annals of the Association of American Geographers*, 66, September 1976.

Motte, Jacob R. in *Journey Into Wilderness*. (Edited by James F. Sunderman). Gainesville: University of Florida Press, 1963, pp. 90-91.

Niles Weekly Register, 2 July 1836; 24 September 1836; 22 October 1836.

Official Records of War of Rebellion, Vol. LIII. Washington: Government Printing Office.

O'Neal, W.R. "Memoirs of a Pioneer." (Orlando) *The Sunday Sentinel Star*, 15 October 1943.

Otto, John. "Open Range Cattle-herding in Southern Florida." *Florida Historical Quarterly*, Vol. XXVIII. St. Augustine: Florida Historical Society, July 1999, pp. 53-65.

Otto, John Solomon, "Florida's Cattle-Ranching Frontier: Hillsborough County (1860)." *Florida Historical Quarterly*, 63. Melbourne: Florida Historical Society, 2003.

Patrick Rembert, (ed.). "Letters of the Invaders of East Florida, 1812." *Florida Historical Quarterly*, Vol. XXVIII. St.Augustine: Florida Historical Society, July 1949, pp. 53-65.

The People of Camden County Georgia. Kingsland: Southeast Georgia, 1982, p. 14.

Pizzo, Tony. "James McKay, The Scottish Chief of Tampa Bay." Tampa *Tribune*, pp. 6-9.

"Reminiscences." (Jacksonville) *The Florida Sun*, 16 September 1876, p. 2.

Shofner, Jerrell H. *Orlando, The City Beautiful*. Orlando: Douglas S. Drown, 1984, pp. 33-35.

Smith, Julia F. *Slavery and Plantation Growth in Antebellum Florida, 1821-1860*. Gainesville: University of Florida Press, 1973.

Stevens, Wallace. "Cattle Kings of Florida." *Atlanta Journal*, 14 December 1930.

"Summerlin Family Reunion." *Bartow Informant*, 27 January 1883, p. 1.

Summerlin, Jacob. "Cattle Sale." (Tampa) *The Sunland Tribune*, 5 October 1878, p. 3.

Taylor, Robert. "Cow Cavalry: Munnerlyn's Battalion in Florida, 1864-1865." *Florida Historical Quarterly*, 65. Melbourne: Florida Historical Society, Oct. 1986.

Taylor, Robert. "Rebel Beef: Florida Cattle and the Confederate Army." *Florida Historical Quarterly*, 67. Melbourne: Florida Historical Society, July 1988.

Taylor, Robert. *Rebel Storehouse*. Tuscaloosa: University of Alabama Press, 2001.

Tebeau, Charlton and Carson, Ruby. *From Indian Trail to Space Age*. Vols. I and II, Delray Beach: Southern Publishing Co., 1965.

The Tampa Daily Times, 23 December 1935; 28 October 1926; 4 November 1926.

Tucker, Cecil A, II. "Indian Paths, Military Roads, and the Cattle Trails of Florida." *Florida Cattle Frontier Symposium, 1845-1995*. Kissimmee: Florida Cattlemen's Association and Florida Cracker Cattle Breeder's Association, 1995.

VanLandingham, Kyle. "Captain William B. Hooker: Florida Cattle King." *Florida Cattle Frontier Symposium, 1845-1995*. Kissimmee: Florida Cattlemen's Association and Florida Cracker Cattle Breeder's Association, 1995.

Jacob Summerlin

VanLandingham, Kyle and Akerman, Joe. *Florida Cattle Kings.* Unpublished manuscript, 1978.

Veterans of Various Wars Buried in Polk County, Florida, Vol. 10. St. Petersburg: September, 1982, p. 144.

"Wills of Alachua County Florida," *Annals of Georgia,* Vol. II. Effingham County Records, 1844-1845, p. 130.

Woods, Thomas. "Plat with Description of Claim in East Florida on Path to Jacob Summerlin's," Vol. I. Tallahassee: Florida State Archives, p. 207.

Wynne Lewis, and Taylor, Robert. *Florida in the Civil War.* Charleston, SC: Arcadia, 2001.

Personal Interviews

Arsdel, Sara Van (Executive Director of Orange County Historical Society, Inc.). Orlando, FL, January 10, 2000.

Bartlett Patricia (Florida historian, former Director of Matheson Historical Center). Gainesville, FL, April 7, 2004.

Bearheart, Micco Bobby Johns (Native American Chief of Perdido Bay Tribe). Tallahassee, FL, April 3, 2004.

Bronson Anna F. (Former cattlewoman and friend of Sam Summerlin). Kissimmee, FL, July 14, 1991.

Brown, Canter (Historical writer and university professor at FAMU). Several interviews about Summerlin family, Tallahassee, FL, 2000-2004.

Brunson, Rick (Desk Editor, Orlando *Sentinel,* Has done considerable research on Jacob Summerlin). Orlando, FL, January 1998.

Carlton, Reuben, III (Florida cattleman). Fort Pierce, FL, December 22, 1975.

Carlton, Wayne Reuben (Florida cattleman). Indian Town and Fort Pierce, FL, December 22, 1975.

Coleman, Carline H. (Genealogist). Gainesville, FL, August 1, 1988.

Ferrell, Tommie (Relative of the Summerlins, Real Estate Development Specialist, Division of Florida Land Sales). Tallahassee, FL. Several interviews from 1976-1995.

Frisbie, Louise (Journalist, publisher and historical writer). Bartow, FL, August 1978.

Glass, Ann W. (Librarian at Moultrie Genealogical Library). Moultrie, GA, July 29, 2004.

Hamlin, Raymond (Charter member of Florida Cracker Cattle Breeders Association and cattleman). Several interviews from January 1, 1999 to February 2003.

Hawk, Robert (Historical writer, Former Director of the Historical Division of the Florida Department of Military Affairs). Several interviews, St. Augustine, FL, 1988 – 2000.

Hendry, Sara Nell (Direct descendant of Captain F.A. Hendry and expert on cattle frontier in Southwestern Florida). Several interviews between 1995 – 2004.

Horn, Helen (Relative of Jacob Summerlin, Junior). Cave Creek, AZ, August 5, 2004.

Johnston, Lela Summerlin (Granddaughter of William Towles and Summerlin relative). Fort Myers, FL, April 27, 1978.

Keuchel, Edward (Historical writer and historical professor at FSU, Author of *A History of Columbia County*). Several interviews, 1996.

Knetsch, Joe (Historian for Florida Department of Environmental Protection Division of State Lands and historical writer). Several interviews, Tallahassee, FL, 1990 – 2004.

Lesley, Theodore (Late Florida historian, possessed several original documents by Jacob Summerlin, Junior). Tampa, FL, January 4, 1976.

Lykes, Charles (Manager of Lykes' cattle operation). January 3, 1976.

Martin, Flora (Direct descendant of Aaron Jernigan). Orlando, FL, February 2, 1977.

Miller, Mrs. Jan (Direct descendant of John Summerlin). Fort Pierce, FL. Several interviews between December 12, 2003 to June 1, 2004.

Moore, Mrs. Polly (Direct descendant of John Summerlin). April 5, 2004.

Odom, Ellen P. (Genealogy Librarian). Moultrie, GA, June 5, 2000.

Parker, Susan (Historian with St. Augustine Preservation Board; Historical writer). St. Augustine, FL, June 10, 2004.

Partin, Mrs. Henry O. (Late widow of Henry O. Partin, cattle rancher). Kissimmee, FL, December 4, 1975.

Prewett, Vickie (Orange County Parks and Recreation). Fort Christmas, FL, December 6, 1999.

Snodgrass, Dena (Historian, teacher and historical writer; friend of Sam Summerlin). Jacksonville, FL, May 10 and 11, 1980.

Starkey, J.B., Junior (Late cattleman). St. Petersburg, FL, October 6, 1975.

Stein, Teresa (Florida Heartland Heritage Foundation). Lake Placid, FL, March 1, 2003.

Tucker, Cecil A., II (Florida cattleman and historical writer). Fort Christmas, FL, Several interviews from December 2000 – June 2004.

VanLandingham, Kyle (Historian; author and attorney). Denver, CO. Several interviews, 2000 – 2004.

Wright, Abner (Late Retired cattleman and former acquaintance of Summerlin family). Arcadia, FL, May 25, 1975.

Index

Fort Davenport, 38
Fort Dulaney, 50
Fort Eagle (near Live Oak, Florida), 14
Fort Gilleland, Newnansville, 14, 20
Fort Macomb, 18
Fort Meade, 40, 41, 54, 55, 59-61, 63, 90, 94, 122
Fort Mellon, 30, 82, 84, 95, 126
Fort Mitchell, 4
Fort Myers, 37, 39, 50, 56, 57, 59, 61, 63, 68, 69, 89-91, 94, 97, 103-106, 122, 123, 130, 131
Fort Ogden, 50, 54, 56, 68, 92
Fort Palmetto, 17
Fort Pierce, 37, 95
Fort Sumter, 49
Fort Taylor, 18
Fort Wheeler, 18
Fort White, 14, 17, 20, 21
Francis A. Hendry's Independent Cavalry Company, 60, 129
Freedman's Bureau of Refugees and Abandoned Lands, 29, 66, 67
Freedman's Bureau schools, 68

G

Gates, [ ], 45
General Worth's Order #27, 35
Geneva, Florida, 80, 95
Godwin, R. A., 129
Godwin, Soloman, 63, 129
Gold doubloons, 67, 91, 96
Green, James, 45, 129
Green, James D., 32, 59
Griffin, John, 58
Groversville, 53
Guillielerrmo, Spanish ship, 99, 100

H

Hagen, Mary Ann, 4, 8
Hamilton, George, 25, 33
Hamilton, James, 63
Hamiltons, 7
Hancock, William, 43
Hanson, Colonel G. A., 110
Harney, Colonel William S., 20
Harris, William Lloyd, 109
Harris, William S., 63

Harrison, William, 20
Hart, Isaiah, 3
Hart, Ossian Bingley, 3, 4, 81, 97, 119
Hassett, Father Thomas, 3
Hayman, J. M., Reverend, 62
Hayman, S. J., 110
Henderson, William B., 45
Hendry, A. J., 129
Hendry, F. A., 45, 50, 52, 54, 55, 59-61, 63, 64, 67, 68, 90, 96, 97, 103, 104, 106-108, 129, 130
Hendry, George W., 129
Hendry, James, 91
Hendry, W. M., 129
Henry, B., 45
Hickory Bluff, 92, 97
Highlanders, 6
Highlands City, 63
Highlands County, 95
Hill, Adam, 110
Hilliards' Island, 20
Hillsborough County, 9, 25, 30-33, 41, 43, 51, 52, 122, 126
Hodges Company, 58
Hog Town (Gainesville), 13
Hogan, F. B., 129
Holden Prairie, 94
Hollingsworth, Sam C., 129
Hollingsworth, W. K., 129
Hollinsworth, Stephen, 39
Holmes, "Teet", 92
Hooker, William, 43, 45, 51, 97, 120
Hopkins, Maj. Gen. B., 39, 40
Hubbard, Daniel, 37
Hughes, Captain David, 69, 110
Hughey, George, 39
Hughey, James, 86
Huntress, Ship, 45

I

Insurrectos, 97
International Ocean and Telegraph Company, 90

J

Jackson, President Andrew, 11
Jackson, General John K., 51
Jackson, J. A., 116

Jackson, Stonewall, 49
Jernigan, Aaron, 39, 79
Jernigan, Isaac, 39
Jernigans, 46, 80
Jessup, General, 18, 19, 95
Johnson, Captain Clay, 106
Johnson, President Andrew, General Amnesty Order, 62
Johnson, Prince (slave owned by Jacob Summerlin, Jr.), 41, 128
Johnston, Captain Abner D., 43, 95, 120
Johnston, Francis, 43
Jones, Micco Bobby "Bearheart", 38
Jones, Sam, 58, 59
Jones, Thomas, 59, 129

K

Kate Dale, ship, 56
Keen, E. B., 129
Kendrick, Captain, 52
Key West, 43, 46, 50, 56, 66, 68, 89, 96, 99, 108, 130
Key West *Democrat*, 107
Kinchreek, T., 39
King of the Crackers, 1, 8, 86, 91, 93, 100, 101, 110-112
Kingsley, Zephaniah, 4
Kissimmee, 20, 30, 97, 103, 105, 106, 111, 115, 123
Kissimmee River, 30, 35, 44, 55, 67, 82, 95, 104-106
Knight, Jesse, 39
Knight, Mary Roberts, 23, 33
Knight, Samuel, 25, 122
Knight's Station, 25, 26, 28, 122

L

Lake Alligator, 5
Lake Conway, 95
Lake Eola, 79, 85, 86, 123
Lake Holden, 79
Lake Monroe, 87, 94, 115
Lake Okeechobee, 17, 103, 104, 105, 106, 123
Lancaster, Joseph B., 5
Lang, David, 4
Lang, Lydia, 4, 121
Lanier, John, 43

Lanier, Louis, 43, 55
Lee, Robert E., 49, 62
Lesley, John T., 45
Leslie, Theodore, 130
Lewis, Bronson (panther attack), 29
Liberty County, Georgia, 67, 109, 123
Livingston, Captain, 17, 19
Long Bluff, early Summerlin property, 2
Longstreet, James, 49, 62
Longwood, Florida, 82, 115
Lopas, Don Justo, 3
Lovell, W. A., 82, 85
Lucky, Sam, 91

M

Madison, Florida, 6, 53-55, 60, 92
Magnolia, ship, 45
Maiden cane, 27, 30
Mamie Lown, ship, 106
Manatee River, 44, 92, 122
Mandarin, Florida, 5
Marion Springs, 36
Marion, General Francis, 5
Matchless, ship, 44
McAuley, John, 64
McBride, A., 58
McCarty, Sarah, 2
McClellan, J. L., 130
McKay, D. B., 8, 9, 15
McKay, James, 44-46, 50, 51, 54, 56, 57, 59, 60, 66, 91, 96, 122
McKay, Richard, son of James and Confederate officer, 56
McKinley, Rev. E. C., 117
McLeland, John, 2
McLellan, George, 19
McMullen, James P., 55
McNeils, 45
Meeks, Henry L., 82
Mellonville (Sanford), 31, 80, 82, 87
Midland Railroad, 115
Mikasuki Indians, 14, 18, 28, 35, 36, 39, 40, 57-59, 61, 90
Mills, Lt. Colonel W. J., 15
Milton, Governor John, 51, 58
Mineral Springs, 17
Mitchell, George W, 129
Mizell, David, 80, 95